THE RELUCTANT MESSERSCHMITT

The author, Don Everson, is a journalist who was born in 1919, educated at Caterham School and studied aircraft design before World War II. He served in the R.A.F. from 1939–46 and learned a great deal about crashed aircraft, having been obliged to examine the remains of over 60 crashes just after the events. During the last 15 years he has written copy for the motor industry, the polymer industry and aeronautics. He has now brought to this book the benefit of his experience together with enthusiasm and a continued interest in aircraft.

The Reluctant Messerschmitt

Don Everson

Published by
PORTCULLIS PRESS LTD.
Queensway House, 2 Queensway,
Redhill, Surrey RH1 1QS

First published in 1978 by Portcullis Press Ltd.
Queensway House, 2 Queensway, Redhill, Surrey, RH1 1QS

© Portcullis Press Limited

ISBN 0 - 86108 - 018 - 1

Printed in England by
Love & Malcomson Ltd.,
Brighton Road, Redhill, Surrey

DEDICATION

To June, without whose help and constant encouragement
this book could never have been written.

FOREWORD

My first-hand acquaintance with the Messerschmitt 109 lasted over a period of nearly five years and, though respectful, was certainly not friendly.

It started, with a bang, over Dunkirk in late May 1940. It developed, not always to my advantage, over London and South East England later that year; became particularly rancorous during endless Fighter Command "sweeps" across Northern France in the summer of 1941 and 1942; continued over Tunisia, Sicily and Southern Italy in the spring and summer of 1943; and fizzled out over Central Italy in the high summer of 1944, as the Luftwaffe was withdrawn from that area to defend the homeland.

On two occasions I was well and truly shot down by Me 109's; on numerous occasions I was peppered; and on countless occasions frightened out of my wits.

In the circumstances it may seem strange that I should have found myself subject to a growing fondness for the reluctant hero of this book. Or perhaps it is not so strange: for the Me 109, like its arch-foe the Spitfire, was not only a superbly efficient fighter plane, but had character and personality of an order which is special and unique to a few of its particular generation of warplanes.

You don't have to love it – though no doubt there are many who did and who do. But you do have to admire it.

I am glad that they got this one up and brought it back in friendship across our coast.

HUGH DUNDAS

ACKNOWLEDGEMENTS

The author wishes to offer his gratitude to all who helped with the continuing search for historical information concerning the finding of "the reluctant Messerschmitt" and in the tracing of the events that led up to the demise of the aircraft.

The author is indebted to Group Captain Hugh Dundas, CBE, DSO, DFC, whose experiences during the Battle of Britain and in other theatres of the war render him eminently fitting as the writer of the Foreword to this book.

Additionally, thanks are offered to Mr F. K. Mason for his helpful comments on the reconstruction of past air battles and for that incredible volume of historical statistics: "Battle over Britain". Very special thanks are also due to Mr. P. D. Cornwell for access to his private collection of historic records, and for his personal interpretation of events over SE England on October 7, 1940.

The author's thanks are also due to three famous members of 501 Sqdn, RAF, namely: AVM H. A. V. Hogan, CB, DFC; W/C E. Holden, OBE, DFC, and W/C K. W. Mackenzie, DFC, AFC, for digging deeply into their personal memories to help sort out the events of thirty-seven years ago.

For much of the German research, the author is indebted to Herr H. Kirchner, who acted as hon. liaison officer in Germany for the Brenzett Museum, and to Herr K. Müller and Herr Victor Mölders who added unique touches with their personal memories of October 7. Special mention must be made of the pilot of the reluctant Messerschmitt, Herr E. Meyer, who provided so many details about the way the new style of fighter bombing started, together with his recollections of the last air battle and final ditching of his aircraft.

For the interpretation of the sequence of events that led up to the strange behaviour of the undercarriage of the Me 109 E4 and for the wartime pilots' handling notes on that aircraft, the author wishes to thank the members of the team at the Royal Aircraft Establishment, Farnborough, Hants. It is a great pity that those concerned cannot be named personally because of the protocol of the Civil Service.

To the two teams of amateurs who made the whole book possible in the first place the author offers his gratitude and wholehearted amazement that their enthusiasm for this unusual venture never ran dry, whatever the problems encountered, over a period of several years. To the two team leaders, Jess Henderson and Dave Buchanan, it is good to see that the ancient arts of leadership are still alive and well in Kent in the year of the Silver Jubilee. To Jess, leader of the Channel divers, special thanks for the initiation into the gentle arts of sea diving and for persuading your bunch of pirates to reveal some of their underwater secrets in the snug at "The Swan". To Dave, leader of the Museum Group, many thanks for always being available when advice and help were needed. May your "Battle of Britain" Museum become a focal point to future generations seeking the truth about an air battle that will remain unique in the historic collection of stories of men at war.

CONTENTS

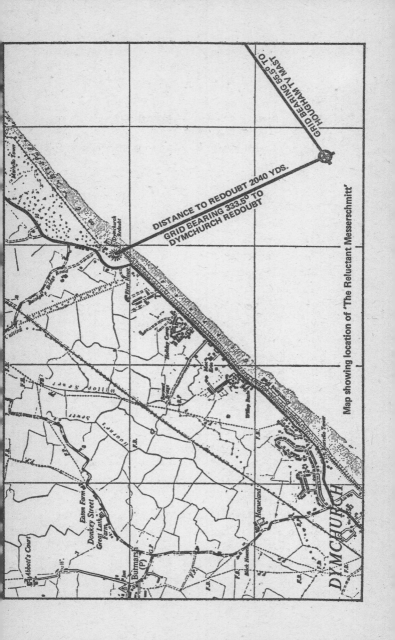

GRID BEARING 55.5° TO
HOUGHAM T.V. MAST

DISTANCE TO REDOUBT 2040 YDS.
GRID BEARING 333.5° TO
DYMCHURCH REDOUBT

Dymchurch Redoubt

Map showing location of 'The Reluctant Messerschmitt'

DYMCHURCH

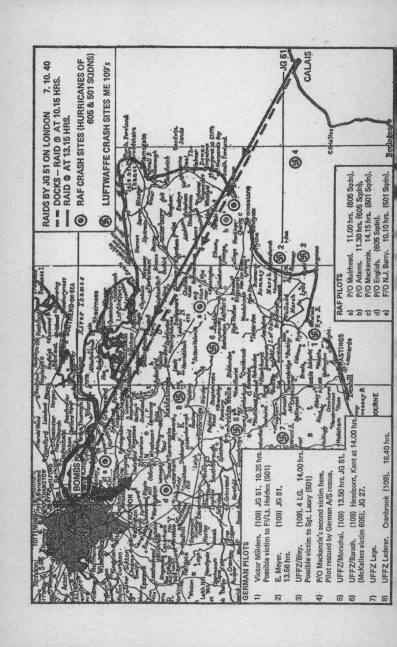

RAIDS BY JG 51 ON LONDON   7. 10. 40

■ ■ ■ DOCKS – RAID ① AT 10.15 HRS.
━━━ RAID ② AT 13.15 HRS.

◎ RAF CRASH SITES (HURRICANES OF
    605 & 501 SQDNS)

卍 LUFTWAFFE CRASH SITES ME 109's

RAF PILOTS

a) P/O Muirhead,   11.00 hrs. (605 Sqdn).
b) P/O Adams,   11.30 hrs. (605 Sqdn).
c) P/O Mackenzie,   14.15 hrs. (501 Sqdn).
d) P/O English,   (605 Sqdn).
e) F/O N.J. Barry, 10.10 hrs. (501 Sqdn).

GERMAN PILOTS

1) Victor Mölders, (109) JG 51. 10.35 hrs.
   Possible victim to Fl/Lt. Holden (501)

2) E. Meyer,   (109) JG 51.
   13.56 hrs.

3) UFFZ/Bley.,   (109), 4 LG. 14.00 hrs.
   Possible victim to Sgt. Lacey (501)

4) P/O Mackenzie's second victim here,
   Pilot rescued by German A/S rescue.

5) UFFZ/Morschal. (109) 13.50 hrs, JG 51.

6) UFFZ/Barsch,   (109) Headcorn, Kent at 14.00 hrs.
   (McKellers victim 605): JG 27.

7) UFFZ Lege,

8) UFFZ Lederer,   Cranbrook (109). 16.40 hrs.

PROLOGUE

To those watching the sky, October 7th 1940 differed little from many other days of the summer. The Battle of Britain had been staged against a bright blue backdrop, a panoramic background for over three months and the initial awe at the spectacle had now reduced, and become almost commonplace to those living in the area of Romney Marsh. The arrival of sudden death on the family doorstep was now an almost everyday occurrence and its familiarity had produced emotions which were akin to sophisticated boredom. The Heinkels and Dorniers would arrive with the milkman and return, usually individually with indecent haste, shedding a wake of burning and broken metal over the Weald of Kent. It was the fact that the milk continued to arrive, and the shops still sold goods from a much reduced range, and that, if so inclined, the farmer could still get to market that had taken the excitement from the war, and reduced it to a level of acceptance, whatever the next day might bring.

October 7 was fine, with cumulus cloud seeding above the South downs, in contrast to the heavy drizzle that had plagued the previous days, as the raiders started to arrive over the coast from the airfields in France. But this day there was a subtle change in the nature of the visitors. The bigger birds were missing.

Instead of formations of the now familiar Heinkels, Dorniers and Junkers with their escort of tiny Messerschmitts, discerning observers could now only see the smaller waves of Me 109's climbing still for the safer operational height of 25,000 ft. Some of the aircraft were seen, through binoculars, to carry an unusual black shape beneath their wings. But the bombers were conspicuous by their absence.

Less than an hour later the tiny fighters returned. This time in a low level rush, many of them with their bellies glued to the contours of the downs to help to evade the pursuing Hurricanes and Spitfires. Those that had not had the luck to escape in this way could be seen from the con-trails in the sky,

11

tracing the pattern of the battle all fighting their way back to the Channel and the safety of the coast of France. Soon, there was nothing for the watcher to see except the smoke of burning wreckage spearing above the crests of the downs to mark the path of the battle.

Three hours later, the wailing of the sirens warned that the pattern of the early raid was to be repeated. Again waves of Messerschmitt fighter bombers and their escorts crossed the coast to the South-East of Folkestone apparently heading for targets in the London area. For those who counted, over sixty aircraft formed a swarm of silver dots with little formal shape. As before, they were still climbing for height, some already well above the lower cloud strata. To the watchers of New Romney, their lunches disturbed by the compulsive act of aircraft identification, the next hour's wait would be uneasy perhaps, but tempered with the thought that again they would not be the target of the Nazi wrath. It was all quite different to the days of June when the Radar and local airfields had been the primary targets.

Today it had to be some one else's turn, and they were relegated to the role of bystander in these acts of war.

At the headquarters of the RAF Fighter Command, this change of enemy tactics had been noted. The early reports from the Royal Observer Corps and the chain of Radar stations around the South coast had all reported the absence of the larger bombers in the first raid and were now busy checking for unsuspected villainy by the Luftwaffe. Were there to be other diversionary raids in other areas and would the main bomber force arrive from a different direction after the fighters had landed and were being refuelled? 501 and 605 Squadrons of 11 Group had already been scrambled from Croydon and Kenley to patrol an area near Biggin Hill to intercept the aircraft, and other 11 Group squadrons were in the process of taking off to back up the defenders. Taken in isolation, there was no logic in the use of Me 109's in this new role. If sixty aircraft crossed to London and 20 of them were equipped with 250 kg bombs and succeeded in dropping them on the London Dock area, as had happened in the first raid of the morning, what was the net result of the act?

Indiscriminate bombing from high altitude from a loose

12

formation had produced a bomb spread of over ten miles in area, with 30% of the bombs falling harmlessly in the river, and apart from the odd lucky hit or two on warehouses, the rest had fallen on civilian property or on open marshland around the docks. Aircraft losses on both sides were still being evaluated, but the first raid had been of no military value to the Luftwaffe, and a second raid of similar proportions made even less sense to the controllers. There had to be a catch somewhere.

At 25,000 ft, S/Ldr McKeller had already found one, when a flight of trigger happy Spitfires had bounced 605 Squadron in error, and the two units were now sorting out the resultant confusion. S/Ldr Hogan who was patrolling his 501 Squadron Hurricanes near to S/Ldr McKeller in the area of Sevenoaks missed this incident, but shortly after both squadrons were vectored onto formations of Me 109's some of which were carrying bombs. Seconds later the rival airforces were at grips high over the English countryside.

Back at the lifeboat stations, and Observer Corps units scattered around the coast of Kent, there were men who were awaiting the outcome of the air battle with professional interest. Members of the ARP units were also watching and awaiting the inevitable incidents that always followed a raid. Observers watching from the hose towers of fire stations were waiting to give the usual running commentary to their colleagues in the stations below. Looking to the North the white and blue confusion of the returning raiders was already visible. Their return was firmly announced by two hedge hopping Me 109's thundering over the ploughland and disappearing out over the sea hotly pursued by a gaggle of Hurricanes firing at their tails. Above and in almost leisurely pace an odd group of three Me 109's scurried out of cloud cover turning slightly to avoid the flack concentrations at Folkestone. One unidentified aircraft could be seen crashing near to the Ashford railway line and was already well on fire before reaching its final resting place.

Both to the East and to the West, observers could see and hear the sounds of air battle and retain short glimpses of posturing Hurricane or Messerschmitt in motion, some trailing white or black smoke as lethal energy was dissipated in the fast emptying skies.

Out to sea, observers saw three aircraft ditch during a period of twenty minutes. Their position and times were firmly logged. The lifeboat at Dungeness was launched and sighting reports sent to the local RAF units. Survivors were taken from the lethal clutches of the cold waters of the Channel, some as prisoners of war and others returned to their respective RAF units to fight another day. The day's only major significance was that it had heralded the start of the night bombing of London. Daylight appearances of the German bombers had produced losses that were too heavy to be sustained. The role of the Me 109 fighter bomber was to be purely to keep the RAF airborne during the hours of daylight, and to reveal to the Chiefs of Staff a gaping hole in its plans for the defence of Britain's cities by night.

The day of October 7 1940 was soon forgotten in the welter of coming events and it was only by chance that it was to be remembered in any detail over 37 years later, when a fisherman caught his nets on the wreckage of one of the fighter bombers.

This book tells the story of the recovery from the sea of the Me 109 and of the reconstruction of both the aircraft and of the history that surrounded its last flight.

PART ONE

1 THE BIG CATCH

"To fall overboard in the Straits, and then come up with a Dover sole in your mouth. That, I call a lucky fisherman."

(*Anon*)

According to local fisherman Alan Griggs, finding fish is forty per cent skill and sixty per cent luck. On June 2, 1974, at about 0200 hours the tide was full at Folkestone harbour, the night very dark and the sea calm.

Those would be the first ingredients of a fisherman's mix of luck and if, like Alan, your way of life was that of a professional fisherman, you might say that the day had a fair start.

Inshore trawling had been Alan's life since he was eighteen. The urge to fish had been deeply inbred and the family could claim to have been fishing for four centuries. He served his apprenticeship on his father's boat, slowly understanding the economics of the sea hunt. That it was not enough to catch fish; they must be landed safely and the right price obtained in the market. The fishing gear must be maintained, the boat seaworthy, with fuel in its tanks for the next day. At seventeen, a brief excursion ashore as a carpenter had left him with a love of tools, and the conviction that inshore fishing would be his only way of life. His father, understanding, had financed his first boat, the "Joan of Arc".

The harbour at Folkestone is tidal and Alan had to

row to his moorings, secure the small boat and climb aboard. At low tide, the "Joan of Arc" was kept upright by her legs, a wooden framework on each side which had to be lifted and secured aboard. She was a small 33 ft two master with diesel engine, a small auxiliary sail and a square wheelhouse amidships. There was also radio. Two side tanks held the fuel which was sufficient for about twenty days at sea, a sea day being normally from high tide to high tide.

Alan's plans for the next twelve hours were routine. First it was necessary to start up the engine, cast off and spend the next hour and a half under way to the fishing grounds. From his chart, he would select the trawl areas to be used that trip. These were lines drawn on the chart based on past experience, and fished with expedience. If visited too often, poor catches would result, so a careful balance had to be maintained. There were also other snags.

Sometimes Alan worked with a crew of one. The job of the extra crew member would be to assist with the nets, with the hauling in of the catch and with its sorting, throwing away the rubbish of marine flotsam, cleaning, gutting and boxing the catch. On this trip Alan had elected to do this work himself. True, there would be no profit to be split, but the workload would be doubled and also require his presence aft, away from the wheelhouse, for lengthy periods during the trip.

Provided the sea and winds were predictable, there was little danger, and with ten years of experience behind him, a fatty rind of caution was present in his movements about the boat. Alan, in common with many other fishermen, could not swim and had little inclination to learn. Inshore fishing could mean being up to ten miles away from land, and there were the usual safety devices aboard: life jackets, pyrotechnics and the like.

On the trip out to the trawl area, his thoughts were divorced from the slow movement of the boat. As a car driver may arrive at his destination without positive recall of his actions, the act of travel was instinctive. Money began to take over his thought process.

With inflation, prices of most things were rising rapidly, and the commodity that gave him his living, the Dover sole, was beginning to fetch market prices that would have shattered his ancestors. In 1974, a catch of thirty fish would mean about 25–28 lb weight. A box of sole weighing about five stone and you were talking about £70 and, during the warm summer nights and early mornings, a catch of three or four boxes might not look a lot in terms of volume, but do this five times a week and you could start to think in terms of a larger boat. Of course, it would have to be on the well tried lines of "Joan of Arc", but with another ten feet of length for a start. Certainly it would need a more powerful engine. The image became clearer. Now here was a boat for all seasons, a boat that cut down the time to get to the trawl areas, and this would mean more fishing time between high tides, for deck space for the boxes and gear, more seabed to be swept . . .

A small, dark vision of discontent nudged its way across the vista of a rapidly growing bank account. Of course, the "Joan of Arc" must be sold – no, part exchanged, for a higher price. Bigger engines meant higher fuel bills and more fish meant much more deck work. Perhaps a partner would help; certainly a regular crew. That would mean shared profits – and where would you get such a crew?

To his schoolmates, Alan remembered, his declaration of faith to a career of inshore fishing had brought some predictable reactions. "You're mad; you come home wet and shivering, stinking to high heaven, spend half your life at the mercy of the tides." Or worse: "Make way for Long John Silver and his grotty parrot. He can't play football – got a wooden leg."

After a time, Alan had given up explaining, and developed his own brand of verbal cynicism to combat the inevitable misconception of a fisherman's way of life. He also knew that the simple laws of economic life governed those ashore with the same inevitability as those at sea. To find crew from his own age group, or younger, meant finding someone who must think as he did about working 12 or 24 hour shifts to maximise the catch.

The vision of the new boat returned. A modern business used modern methods, and now there was Radar and such things as a Decca navigator to cut out the guesswork in navigation. Yes, that was the thing. Mind you, you couldn't buy them. The company would hire them to you and give you a crash course in their technicalities, but you just looked at the intersection of the red and green lanes on the special chart and there was your position within 30 feet or so.

The thoughts of position finding brought Alan back to the job in hand. His time, course and speed, combined with his knowledge of the tides, brought him the certainty that he was nearly at the spot to start the trawl. The sky was showing the false light that comes before the dawn. The Sovereign Light and other inshore lights confirmed his position before he commenced the work of getting the nets over the side.

On "Joan of Arc" the main winch for the nets was located amidships. The nets themselves were some 60 feet in length and had two main attachment points with a dual spread of additional wires attached to otter boards slung at an angle so that they came along the boat's bottom holding the trawl rope. They were capable of taking a strain of up to twenty tons well spread, but the normal loading would rarely exceed three tons. Nets were expensive and made for durability rather than high load bearing. Below water, the weighted trawl line took the net down, and once on the sea bed kept part of the net in contact with the sea bottom on the end of the 40-foot warps, the net itself swelling out like an inflated balloon. All that the fisherman needed now was the presence of the fish.

On deck, Alan felt the change in trim of the boat caused by the drag of the nets. This, and the speed of the boat, could be compensated with an increase of power. The scavenging action of the nets on the sea bed brought not only fish but an additional problem in navigation. This was the hazard of old wrecks.

Some of these are clearly marked on the charts. Some are not. The fishermen who travel the same trawl lanes know of many underwater items that never appear in official charts, and treat them with due respect. Once a net has been caught on an unexpected obstacle, the news travels like wildfire in the fishing fraternity, and small private marks duly appear on the charts of the small boats. One such mark appeared on the chart that Alan used and he always treated it with great respect. It had the reputation among the fishermen of being a real bastard. With some obstructions you could, with skill and a friendly tide, contrive to manoeuvre your net free.

Not so with this one. You could say goodbye to your net and £70.

The first sweep was without incident and during the second sweep Alan could feel the change in the trim of the boat with the tide moving with the net.

It was now almost dawn, bringing with it a fresher inshore wind. Alan's mind went back to the image of his new boat. He would, he decided, christen it the "Opportunity". He thought about the name. True, it was sexless, but it clearly reflected his intentions for the future. If spoken slowly, the name rolled off the tongue and gave certain direction to the speaker's thoughts. As if sensing this crass lack of loyalty, the "Joan of Arc" began to slow up, and then stopped, its tiny propeller churning without effect on the boat's movement, its blades impotently turning at the same area of water, converting the energy to steam by cavitation.

If Alan had had a crew with him at that moment, they would almost certainly have been blamed. Not that they would have been at fault, for the navigation of the boat was certainly Alan's responsibility. Life being what it is, the human necessity to express feeling at a moment of crisis is a time-honoured and much used maritime prerogative. Being crewless, Alan remained silent, although accurate measurement of torsional stresses of his hands on the ship's wheel would have revealed an unexpected input of about 70 lbs.

He could have sworn that he had allowed just clearance for a known hazard. By entering a series of delicate manoeuvres with power and steering he slackened the starboard net wires in an effort to dodge the boat clear.

It remained resolutely fast. He applied a little power. Not too much, because a combination of side forces, wind, tide and power could overturn a small boat very quickly. The net remained fast. Resigned to the inevitable, he decided to jettison the net. He attached a small plastic orange buoy to the trawl line, and released the shackles retaining the net.

Freed of its harness, the "Joan of Arc" began to behave predictably. Alan took the boat well clear of the obstruction and automatically set about the task of redeploying the spare net. He had been at sea for only two and a half hours, which left him a good eight hours' fishing before returning to harbour.

At the end of the day's fishing, a new net had to be obtained from his store, ready for the next trip. This, and the other routine work completed, Alan made his way ashore again and made for his local pub. He was formulating a plan as he walked: the loss of £70 for a net was an unacceptable loss to a man who was to apply modern methods to fishing. The act of buoying the net had been, in its way, an act of defiance to the fate that had put his boat on the wrong spot, at the wrong moment; certainly not an act to warn other ships of a hazard to trawling.

Alan considered the nature of the underwater obstruction. Local talk and opinion had nominated an old wartime mine cradle. The mine would be long gone leaving the solid based anchorage and metal rod that secured the mine cable to its base. After his recent encounter, Alan was unsure of this identification. From his charts he knew that the high water depth was 50 feet and low water about 35 feet. It couldn't have been a large boat, because Her Majesty's Hydrographers would have certainly noted its position on the chart. Had it been a recent wreck, then all the fishermen would have known about it. Perhaps it was something left over from the D Day flotsam; an old tank, or even part of the Mulberry harbour which hadn't made it to beaches in Normandy. Perhaps it was an old aircraft.

From the direction of the pulls on his net, Alan felt that he had caught in at least two places. Perhaps the propeller blades from an old aircraft?

Whatever the obstruction, Alan knew that this mental investigation of the possibilities was largely academic. Nets that got caught did not usually free themselves, and he, a non swimmer, was certainly not going to dive overboard and try to find them.

The words "dive overboard" caused Alan's face to crinkle in the throes of recollection. What was his name? That local chap he met at Hythe the other week. Said he ran a small group of amateur divers, who were on the lookout for old wartime aircraft that had come down in the sea. Jeff, no, Jess Henderson . . . Now if they could be persuaded to make a dive or two. After all, they were amateurs and would probably be quite happy to have a go if he gave them a drink afterwards. None of that professional £100 an hour nonsense.

He resolved to give Jess a ring that weekend and proposition him. Not that he could say it *was* an aircraft, but, equally, he wasn't certain what it was. Perhaps a gentle hint of aircraft and the laws of probability. That should do the trick.

2 THE DIVERS

"The official manual for sea diving has close on 800 pages of detailed information for the professional and amateur alike. Two-thirds of this work is given over to the dangers of diving and the medical treatment of its victims."

(*Book review*)

Friday, June 1974

When Alan made his 'phone call to Jess Henderson, he kept the details of his problem down to a minimum. He simply said that he had lost a net on an underwater obstruction which could be an old mine cradle or even an old wartime aircraft. Would the lads like to try and free the net? Jess Henderson's first reaction was cautious: "Where is the net, and in what sort of depth of water?" Alan said, "It's in about seven fathoms and about two miles south of the Redoubt, off Hythe. I buoyed the net so you won't have any problem finding it by yourselves."

Jess thought about the problems for a moment before replying. If the net was at forty odd feet, the divers' problems were not complicated by considerations of depth limitations. If indeed it was only two miles off shore, then boat time to and from the diving spot would be fairly short, so not too much fuel would be used. Also it was near enough to the shore for the divers to get clear if the weather changed suddenly. The group could do with a training dive or two on a practical objective, and if it did turn out to be an old wreck site, well, that could be something else.

"We'll try next weekend, if the weather looks right," he said.

23

Even if Jess had known that his reply would commit his club members to most of their spare weekends for the next three years, his answer would almost certainly have been the same. The Hythe Group of Channel Divers was only one of many amateur sub-aqua groups operating round the coast whose diving skills varied inversely with the club leadership and the staying powers of the club members.

Training for the group members took place in the old Scout hut and in the local swimming pool, and when members reached the practical standards required, then they put their new found skills to use at sea. Jess was considered by his club members to be an experienced and enthusiastic leader who believed in the precept of not asking members to do anything he could not already do himself with a large margin of safety. Club rules during diving operations were strict and usually respected, although inexperienced members had been known to ask if all that caution was really necessary. Jess's reply would have certainly been on the lines of: "Try not to find out the hard way. If you get into trouble, then another member will certainly have to get you out of it, and it will be him I'm more worried about."

To the skilled amateur, a lot of diving is pure technique and inevitably judged on this basis. If a diver is sloppy in his technique, then it is likely that his training has been slipshod and, if visiting another club, the diver would certainly be regarded with some suspicion as an underwater companion where interdependence of a high standard is vital.

The Hythe club had a regular Friday night 'phone-in session at Jess's home during the diving season, and members were briefed for the first dive on the net.

The rendezvous was to be Brewers Hill, at Sandgate, where the main road ran close to the beach. Its popularity was derived from a viewpoint of accessibility (diving equipment is heavy) and because the shingle beach shelves gently to about 20 feet. This made it easy to launch the two inflatable boats to be used.

Normally, each diver brings his own equipment, which consists of a wet suit, hood, back pack for the air cylinder (normally an aluminium 55/60 cu. ft Luxfer), mask, demand valve, fins and snorkel. He also has a weight belt to which he can attach lead weights to keep him at the required degree of buoyancy, an underwater watch, a diving knife, and a life jacket, which is usually worn under the body pack. Opinions vary as to what to wear under the wet suit, but diving trunks and wet suit socks are usually considered correct. Protective gloves are also worn when working underwater.

The weather that Sunday was fine, with a fresh inshore breeze and good visibility. The two inflatables took six divers out to sea in the direction of the rather rough position that Alan had passed to Jess. The orange buoy marking was easy to spot, but Jess and Alan's idea of two miles didn't seem to correspond at all, and a number of orange plastic buoys were found in the area.

The first that the group dived on proved to be a whelking buoy. The second buoy was given a hefty exploratory tug from the surface and presented the divers with another fair bag of whelks. The third wouldn't shift, but there was a marked reluctance to be first down to confirm or deny. The contents of an air bottle is precious and its usage would confine the diver to the surface for the rest of the trip. Eventually a buoy was located and the net was clearly visible to the diver after descending about six feet. If part of a net is caught on a seabed obstruction, then the net will billow out like a half inflated balloon and occupy a great deal of sea space around its point of attachment.

When the divers did not surface quickly, they were joined by the others who had realised that something was up. They found that they could pull themselves down the net sides to the seabed, and they also found that the visibility underwater was in the range of three to four feet only, which is equivalent to being out at night in a thick fog, and not at all conducive to underwater salvage.

The salvage plan for the net was fairly simple: one diver stayed in the boat to watch out for other ships and to keep check on the underwater times on each diver. One diver would act as standby diver on the sea bed watching for problems, the other divers worked in pairs trying to free the net. If a diver's back-gear got caught up in the net, the immediate action was to undo the harness from the air bottle, lift the bottle over the head and then unhook the net. Once free, the bottle was returned to its harness. This was quite easy to do under water, so long as the diver kept his head.

The drill for clearing the entangled netting was to run the hands over the net toward the obstruction, pulling the strands together, and then cutting the net clear.

Jess began to take a closer look at the obstruction and found that the net had got hooked up at two points that were clearly the undercarriage legs of a small aircraft. By standing between the two legs he could see that the oleos were still shining silver, but both wheels had gone. Moving back a few feet, Jess felt that he was walking on metal, but his movement ended abruptly when he backed into something flat and hard. Close examination showed it to be about three-quarters of a propeller blade, the rest being deeply embedded in the sand and defying identification.

Jess lost interest in the net completely at that point. He swam round to the other divers and with sign language explained that they had located a crashed aircraft. The net freeing exercise was abandoned, the divers climbed up the buoy line to the inflatables and commenced the routine task of getting aboard.

So long as the diver surfaces close to the boat, this task follows a set drill. The diver hands over his weight belt first, and then hands over his bottle equipment and, finning hard in a downward direction, pulls upward at the same time on the side of the boat. On an inflatable the sides are low in the water and a good heave or two gets him inside the boat.

On the way back to shore, the heavy chatter started. Two undercarriage legs and a bit of propeller wasn't much to go on. Nationality and age were other unanswered problems. If it was a military aircraft, how did one go about claiming it for salvage? Was the cockpit still occupied and was the aircraft still armed?

The one thing that was agreed was that the wreck had got to be brought back ashore if it was at all possible, and the help of the Brenzett Aeronautical Museum had to be sought with a view to doing a combined salvage operation. Jess was duly declared operations manager and chief can-carrier for the Hythe group. He also now had a small aircraft, 90 per cent buried, underwater at forty feet, about a mile and a half offshore from the coast between Sandgate and Dymchurch, and a welter of impractical ideas on how it was going to be brought ashore.

Back in 1973, the divers had established a working relationship with a group of aeronautical archaeologists who had started a small museum on the Romney Marshes near Brenzett. As Jess put it, as far as could be established, all their spare time was spent digging up pieces of crashed aeroplane, finding out who had crashed it and then putting the pieces, suitably labelled, into the museum. Not unnaturally, the pieces that they found were usually rather on the small side and distorted by deceleration. They told the divers that probably the only surviving wartime aircraft were those that had ditched in the Channel between 1940 and 1946 and had simply sunk to the bottom, more or less intact. To salvage such a prize for the museum, it was suggested, might be accomplished if the divers were interested in using their unusual skills in a joint enterprise. Now this was all very well, but most of the divers had been born well after the Battle of Britain and their hobby was diving, not aeroplanes, although they admitted that the odd treasure ship that might have come to the underwater attentions of the club, had they been so lucky, would certainly have been a boon to boosting club funds. Up to that time, they hadn't found any underwater aircraft, and even if they did it would be more likely to contain unexploded bombs than pieces of eight.

The finding of a wartime aircraft suddenly became a challenge to the divers.

Once ashore, the first step was to contact the museum. The curator, David Buchanan, seemed very cheered with the news and suggested that one of his members might come along on the next dive to try and prove the identification of the 'plane so that the necessary authorities could be notified and a claim to ownership legally established. Len Green, vice president and one of the museum experts, agreed to go out with the divers the following Sunday.

With a view to providing the divers with a bit more muscle, experience and inflatable footage for the future, Jess contrived to press-gang all three virtues in the form of one Graham Hayes (hereinafter known as Big Graham), who lived near Canterbury. Big Graham was 47, an experienced member of the Dover sub-aqua club and a Judo brown belt. He ran his own business, having survived twenty-seven years of the motor trade, and he also had the great virtue of owning his own inflatable boat.

The next dive provided quite a flotilla of small boats; even Alan Griggs, the fisherman, brought along the "Joan of Arc" to make sure that Jess found the buoy again and remembered to bring his net up. To his mind, the divers had got quite besotted with a barnacle encrusted bit of old metal they chose to describe as an aeroplane.

Len Green from the museum turned up amongst the first arrivals for the dive the following Sunday. In his early forties, Len had lived in the Hawkinge area as a boy and saw many aircraft shot down in the area during the Battle of Britain and in the war years that followed. This awakened a lasting interest in aircraft and led to him joining the museum staff at a much later date. Being of slim build and gentle disposition, Len did not talk much and probably felt a bit nervous at first with the divers, most of whom looked as if they had been selected from the front row of a Twickenham pack and were bursting with rude health and exuded confidence at every pore. To make matters worse, Len had come down to the beach dressed in a jacket, trousers, shoes and socks, which also seemed to amuse the divers. However, they persuaded him to leave his shoes and socks on the beach, and someone found him an all-enveloping oilskin. Having done that much, the divers then got him aboard Big Graham's boat and went off to their own inflatables to get a ringside view of his initiation into sea travel, sub-aqua style.

Jess thought that Len looked a bit unhappy as they put to sea, and the impression was confirmed on the way out as the inflatable commenced to ship large quantities of sea water and spray over the reluctant passenger. According to the divers, Len didn't say a word on the way out to the marker buoy, where they met up with the "Joan of Arc".

When diving commenced, Jess and Graham (Little) went down and started on the task of gathering and freeing the net. When it was clear of the obstruction, they brought up the trawl line for Alan to hitch onto the ship's winch. The inflatables and divers stood off the area, mainly in the interests of self-preservation, whilst the little trawler started a circular course as the net was hauled in over the side.

Just to show Len that he hadn't been forgotten, the divers

passed over several odd bits of metal that had been lying around on the sea bed. Len became very interested in a small plug of the connector type, and forgot about his wet clothes for a bit. He looked at the plug for a very long time, savouring every part of it, and when the divers were just beginning to think that they ought to go down and bring up something else, he eventually said, "It's almost certainly German." He then lapsed back into a contemplative silence.

This positive identification of the aircraft, together with the recovery of the net, seemed as good a time as any for a tea-break and Alan was duly instructed to do the honours. Up to that moment Alan had been looking ruefully at his net and mentally calculating the number of repairs necessary to make good the damage done by the divers' knives. Muttering darkly about "a mob of knife-happy pirates", Alan returned to the wheelhouse, emerging some minutes later with a large cupful of an evil looking brew. Jess said that the cup had to be shared between four divers and he drank his sitting up in the water.

After the tea-break, the divers tried taking a trawl line from the undercarriage of the wreck to Alan's trawler. They all floated around from various vantage points to see if there was any sign of movement from the air-frame when the trawl line went taut, but maximum power from the "Joan of Arc" failed to produce more than an underwater quiver from the line and no sign of any sand being dislodged from around the imprisoned wreck. Clearly the sea had no intention of giving up its captive without a long struggle.

Back on shore that evening, the news about the find had already reached the curator of the museum via Len Green, and a meeting was arranged for the two clubs at the Duke's Head at Ham Street. Even Alan Griggs became interested in this non-commercial venture, and came along to see if he could help. So, over pints of Kentish ale, a formal agreement was worked out between the two clubs to salvage, beach and restore the aircraft for the museum.

Naturally speculation was high on the aircraft type, and the museum members were all in favour of the wreck being a Messerschmitt 109 of as yet unknown mark. The narrow undercarriage spread suggested attachments at the fuselage and wing junction, and the single airscrew blade could probably be part of a three-bladed propeller. This would tie up nicely with the design detail of the Me 109. From existing data on the aircraft, it was possible to calculate the approximate area that the wreck occupied, assuming it was in one piece, and also the depth that it would be necessary to excavate to free it from the clutches of the sea bed.

In terms of sheer weight, it could be estimated that the aircraft would weigh around 4,200 lbs and the musum would have to think in terms of flotation gear to carry in excess of this figure. Assuming the aircraft could be made buoyant by use of air bags, then it could be floated and towed ashore by a small boat. Once beached, it would be lifted onto a lorry and taken to a suitable store for cleaning and reclamation.

For the divers, Jess said that the wreck was positioned and buoyed somewhere between one and two miles roughly southeast of Dymchurch Redoubt. He thought the weight estimate to be very optimistic as, almost certainly, after thirty-four years underwater the wreck would be full of sand. The aircraft was almost totally submerged in what appeared to be a sand bed, and might have to be dug out to a depth of 6 feet to get it clear for lifting. The divers had little experience of underwater digging and although the fairly shallow sea bed (40 feet) was in their favour, visibility was not, and everything would have to be done by touch, which would compound their difficulties. Lights were no use underwater as, in that sort of visibility, most of the light reflected back in the eyes of the operator. One thing was certain: the digging would be very hard work; diving was for six months of the year only and even then could be very dependent on suitable weather. Work could only be done at weekends, by a small team, and could easily go on for two years. It was also going to involve considerable expense in terms of air bottles and fuel. Additionally, the wreck was uncomfortably close to the army firing range.

Eventually it was agreed that the museum would pay for the divers' air and fuel, Alan Griggs got a contract to tow the aircraft ashore when ready, and the museum also agreed to look into ways of clearing the debris, investigate and claim the title of the wreck and take over the responsibility of the aircraft once it was ashore.

Operation Me 109 was under way.

3 THE MUSEUM

"The nearest some people ever get to gardening is digging up the past."

(Anon)

The Romney Marsh area of Kent is flat, very boggy in parts and full of drunken English lanes. Historically, it has always been considered a suitable landing area for the armies of the militant foreign powers from Rome, France and, much more recently, by Germany. For a Southern area of England it is thinly inhabited, with unexpected farmhouses, old churches and dwellings cropping up usually on the edge of ditches. Pubs are few and the local inhabitants are universally great walkers. The main occupation seems to be sheep breeding, which has the full approval of the sheep, who multiply in great numbers. In the past, battles have been fought on the nearby sea and on the marsh itself. In 1940 a great many more battles were fought in the air over the marshland, many of them ending quickly and tragically for the occupants of the aircraft concerned. During the middle stages of the war, two advance airfields grew up amid the lush meadows and dykes of the marshes. During the last year of the war, the marshland saw the introduction of a massive anti-aircraft belt that stretched from the North Foreland as far west as Portsmouth. This gun belt was largely instrumental in defeating the flying bomb menace that plagued

31

Southern England and London. After the war finished, the beaches were cleared of mines, the miles of barbed wire and concrete pill boxes were removed, and the flotsam of war, drifting through the Channel, disappeared to the sea bed for a final resting place. Slowly, Romney Marsh returned to its pre-war sleep. It was not a place for property speculators, except near the sea shores themselves. An airfield and a nuclear power station grew around the diamond that was Lydd and, as in ages past, sheep farming continued apace and, as a special dispensation to the airfield, a few new and straighter roads scarred the marsh face for the convenience of the travellers and the power station workers.

For perhaps a further twenty years, the marshlands slumbered on. The big stories of the war were told and retold and eventually became the boring point of the next two generations of growing men and women. They wanted and found their own lives in their own style of clothes, of music and of freedom of speech. Through the new medium of television, they became politically awake. They sought power, social power by demonstration, money by strikes; the establishment became a dirty word for many and the now declining armed forces a little bit of a giggle. War in Korea and Vietnam did not touch them except as a demonstration point for the left wing supporters. World War Three was an impossibility, thanks to a balance of atomic power rendering the major nations impotent to strike at one another, for such a move left nothing for anyone to win, if indeed wars can be said to be won.

Curiously, with the passing of time, some memories survived. The great popularity of the RAF Battle of Britain displays every September drew hundreds of thousands of spectators of all age groups, many of them seasoned travellers of the Jet Age, to look again at aviation history drawn from an ancient mix of Spitfires, Hurricanes, Lancasters, Ansons and stringbags. Here was colour and noisy spectacle without the underlying ugliness that was the inevitable product of war.

Survivors of the battle were brought back to face the television cameras as folk heroes for hero-worshipping schoolboys and schoolgirls. The revival of interest in wartime aircraft seemed to trigger off worldwide the start-up of a

32

number of museums for vintage and veteran aircraft. If the aircraft could still fly, so much the better; if not, then the search was on for spare parts.

During 1968, an unexpected flock of Heinkels and Messerschmitts were discovered in Spain and pressed, creaking, into service for the film "Battle of Britain". After the filming was completed, high prices were paid for these war time relics that became dispersed in air museums throughout the world. The cost of building up and maintaining these museums was astronomical, but the public came in their hundreds of thousands to see these relics.

About the same time there came into being very small groups of amateurs, motivated by a mixture of nostalgia, curiosity and enthusiasm, and usually very hard up for ready cash. They researched known crash sites from the wartime period and then dug up the remains of aircraft, often found in the most peculiar of places. From the remains, they painstakingly tried to reconstruct the actual history of each aircraft. These groups could be called the first of the "aeronautical archaeologists".

The Brenzett Aeronautical Museum, situated on Romney Marsh, was formed from two such groups in 1972. As David Buchanan, curator of the museum, said: "Everything happened rather slowly from way back in 1969."

David's interest in aircraft was lifelong. As a boy he had watched aircraft and read all the books he could find on the subject. The interest remained as he grew older, but his occupation did not bring him into contact with the aircraft industry. During 1969 he met the Hukins family based at New House Farm, Biddenden. They found that they had a mutual interest in old aircraft, and David was invited to help them with a "dig" going on at the farm. The aircraft had been of wartime vintage and had made a bad belly landing. A number of odd bits and pieces came to light, but nothing of real significance. No doubt the military authorities had done all the critical salvage at the time of the crash.

They did a bit more research on the next site at Rolvenden, and found that the aid of a mechanical digger was a considerable asset. About this time they decided to form a group and named themselves "The Tenterden Aircraft Recovery Group". The title enabled them to put the digs on an official basis and give credibility to the necessary paperwork. Funds were nil, but members paid 5s. a week into the kitty and, when they accumulated enough, they had a dig. In Kent and Sussex there was no shortage of possible sites to be researched from the war.

About the same time, David said that there was a man named Eric Boswell and some other enthusiasts doing similar work in the Ashford area. This small group had got as far as thinking about a museum to put the results of the digs into some sort of order. Cash was also short here and it was the most natural thing that the two groups, having identical interests, should merge funds and exhibits into a joint museum.

So, in 1972, the Brenzett Aeronautical Museum was founded. As a building it was far from ideal. Originally built as a Women's Land Army hostel during the "Dig for Victory" phase of the war, its structure was typically prefabricated in a T-shape. The group had the offer of the entire building, but some of the roofing was in very poor condition, money was short, so they settled for a part that had once been the old wash house for the land girls. It was said that some of them still came over to look at the old building out of wartime nostalgia, leaving messages like – "Fanny Adams used to work here, please ring" – followed by a phone number, for museum staff members.

The group duly repaired and redesigned the interior of the old buildings and, with the assistance of a lot of white emulsion paint, made a very presentable job that was ideal for wall cases, with the larger exhibits like engines on display down the hut centre. A signboard was duly erected over the front door, some handbills printed, and they were in business as the Brenzett Aeronautical Museum.

The groups had agreed that the whole project was to be a non-profit making scheme, with a proportion of the museum takings going to three carefully selected charities. Special emphasis was laid here on contributions to the Royal Air Force Benevolent Fund. Manning of the museum had to be done by group members when the museum was open at weekends from Easter to October. During July and August, the museum was also open on three additional afternoons, and members and their wives all helped in the establishment of a special place where the public could look with a mixture of wonder and awe at these relics of the "Battle of Britain" and read the carefully collated histories of the exhibits.

New members were recruited from friends and workmates. David said that they had no difficulty in obtaining applicants to join the group. Initially, people were mad keen to come out and help on the "digs", but when it came to sorting out the bits at the store, or joining the rosta for museum duty, then it became surprising how many fell by the wayside. A duty day at the museum starts at 11 a.m. and goes on till 6 p.m., and this can be a bit hard on members' families with seven or eight summer weekends gone effectively on helping an archaeological charity. Members were joined on the clear understanding that they offered voluntary help. Once the commercial side came into things, the project lost something special.

If the museum trades an aircraft part to another museum, the sale proceeds go into the kitty for further work – either digs or research. David said that this did not often happen. People talk about all the exhibits being worth a fortune. The museum are still waiting for these offers of fortunes to appear. The money side is a bit like stamp collecting. If you want to buy, then it's worth a fortune; if you want to sell, then it's worth nothing.

When the group decided to do a dig, work was usually allocated out according to the available talents within the group. David said that his qualifications of administration and a happy knack of getting on with people usually resulted in him getting the job of going to see the difficult farmers. After all, if you intend going into a farmer's field and tearing large chunks out of the ground, then a large chunk of diplomacy is a fundamental basis for the start up of negotiations.

The man doing the current research for the group is John Elgar Whinney. David said, "He spends hours out on the marsh tracking stuff down and then goes home and translates his researches onto maps. He has the characteristics of the bulldog breed and won't give up easily. He just works on until he is sure that there is nothing there, or until the site has been properly cleared up. He also has a good eye for sorting the bits and pieces of crashes together, a most useful art which takes a great deal of experience and patience, most pieces being bent, torn or mutilated way beyond normal recognition."

Much of the information about the site of old wartime crashes comes from eye-witnesses. The researchers have to be very wary here as the information is invariably unreliable. This stems from two basic traits of human behaviour, for although the informant is always full of good faith, details about the crash tend to become distorted or exaggerated with the passing of time and, secondly, people's memory of distances seems to be badly at fault.

They can take you to crash sites that they know well. They will line up and position the sites fairly accurately, but when it comes to the measure of the distance, say from the hedge, then nine times out of ten their judgment will lead them to mark out a spot that is well short of the real site. Naturally, with the passing of thirty-six years or more, the ground gives away nothing in the form of visible clues. The site has to be dug and the distance down can be dependent on the vertical component of the crash, if any, and the rate of overgrowth on the soil (three inches per year in some places). Rocks, chalk or clay all make a considerable difference. If the soil is easily waterlogged, then the diggers will certainly have to use pumps during the wreckage recovery. There again, the size of the aircraft has to be taken into consideration. A 45° impact from a bomber will have spread wreckage all over the area and the heavier parts will usually be further down.

The identification of the nationality of the wreck is often given wrongly by an informant, but the group became very experienced in identifying both nationalities and aircraft types at an early stage in the dig. The metal used in the construction of German aircraft is distinctive, and whilst the British Hurricane, Spitfires and Defiant are closely matched, the thickness of the perspex used in the cockpit canopy construction gives an immediate clue to the country of origin.

Sometimes the most reliable sources can be wrong. A local policeman gave the group details of a crash that happened in 1942. The aircraft, an Me 109, dived vertically from 20,000 feet into the chalk in the North of Kent. Not unnaturally, it dug a deep hole leaving little for the wartime salvage team to find and, after removing certain documents, they filled in the hole and left the remains to rot.

The museum group felt that this unsalvaged site might provide some good specimens and, in order to locate the crash spot accurately, they used a helicopter to get aerial photographs using infra-red photo techniques. The site was pinpointed exactly and, after permission had been obtained, a dig was put in hand. At about twelve feet down confirmation was obtained by the finding of the rudder mass balances.

When the dig reached twenty feet, they came across part of the engine reduction gears, two pistons and a portion of broken crankshaft. After that there was nothing left. The museum staff were puzzled, but the mystery was solved in the local pub where further information was forthcoming. It seemed that an army camp had been based about ¼ mile from the crash site during 1942 and, to help the long summer evenings pass, the soldiers had redug the carefully filled-in site and winched up all the metal parts that remained – on an unofficial basis, of course. The making of cigarette lighters from scrap was a favourite occupation at this time.

This business of collecting souvenirs during wartime became an almost universal practice and most homes could boast of small, and sometimes large, artefacts that had served as a personal reminder to a nearby wartime incident.

When the Brenzett Museum opened, people came from far and wide bringing bits of aeroplane for exhibits, usually complete with a history of sorts. One local character called D-Day White actually brought in a large piece of the wing of an Me 110. The museum staff were rather intrigued with the excellent state of preservation of the exhibit and, under pressure, the donor, a local fisherman, admitted to having trawled up the wreckage. Unfortunately he couldn't recall just where.

The wreckage also had a rack for oxygen bottles, but no bottles, although the clips looked as though they might have been in use very recently. The mystery of the missing bottles was cleared up when a museum member found some in a local antique shop where the owner was selling them to other members of the antique fraternity.

But it was the condition of the wreckage that gave rise to the hope that the museum might do well to try and salvage aircraft that had come down in the sea.

During the war, many aircraft had ditched safely, the crew

taken off by lifeboat and the 'plane just went to the seabed virtually undamaged. The museum had no means of knowing what damage would be done by thirty-four years' immersion, quite apart from storm damage and so on, but the condition of this piece of wing gave rise to hopes of the salvaging of perhaps a complete aircraft – assuming they could find one. The real problem came in trying to get a wreck ashore. The cost would probably be prohibitive, and it wasn't until some of the divers came over to the museum that a possible solution was found. The divers were very keen to have a go and when the news came through from Len Green that here was a complete aircraft, admittedly buried and under water but almost certainly German, the challenge was accepted.

4 THE UNDERWATER DIG

The summer weekends of 1974 were a fairly mixed bag. In the main part the sea was choppy, but not too rough to prevent diving on the aircraft. Curiously, diving visibility went up to almost five feet with these conditions and dropped to two to four feet when calm. Most weekends the diving team would be made up by Jess, Graham (B), Graham (L) and Derek, with odd members of the club coming along to take a look at the aircraft and lend a hand in clearing the site.

The inflatables would start from Hythe, swing out to sea for two miles to avoid the army firing ranges, and then swing back in through 90° to get to the marker buoy. The initial plan was to dig up the sand all round the area occupied by the aircraft, down to a depth of about six feet. None of the divers had actually tried to dig out anything underwater before, so their approach to the problem was totally conventional. They brought along small hoes and hand trowels. Graham (B) thought he would try a garden spade and apply the ordinary agricultural principles. He said, "It didn't work that way at all so I found that I had to go on my knees to get any leverage. You got the blade of the spade in and made a sort of slow sweeping motion away from the aircraft. If you placed yourself right, the underwater current took the sand away from the wreck." Jess tried a modified garden spade with a 4 in. blade and a good sweeping arm action. This worked after a fashion, but when the digging got down about 6 in., the divers found a new problem in the form of hard blue clay. This really slowed up the digging rate. The divers found that they had to add weight to their body belts to prevent the effort generated to dig down being converted into energy which removed them from the digging spot. Graham (B) said that at the start of the dig he carried 16 lbs of body belt weight, and by the end of the '74 season he had had to double the weight.

It was about mid-July that the divers were able to obtain a positive identification of the aircraft. The uncovering of the exhaust stubs revealed a somewhat corroded Daimler Benz 601 Aa liquid cooled engine, which typed the aircraft as almost certainly an Me Bf 109 E4. They had also uncovered the top of the bomb mounting gear between the undercarriage legs, which had at some time retained a 551 lb bomb. The divers had a cautious search around the site for traces of a bomb. Nothing was found, or rather felt, in view of the poor visibility, except some odd lengths of trawl chain which confirmed that other fishermen had been less lucky than Alan in the past.

There were two underwater panics during the 1974 diving season and Jess had to confess that the first panic occurred when he was doing a Sunday morning underwater session. A pressure wave from an underwater explosion slapped hard at his air bottle. Sound is better adapted to underwater travel than in air so the shock from this totally unexpected pressure wave made an immediate ascent to the diving boat obligatory. Divers getting too near to sound or pressure wave sources can suffer severe injury or even death. Nothing had been seen or heard by the others in the boat, who were inclined to be a bit dubious about the whole thing until, the following Sunday, Graham (B) had the same experience, coming up to the surface and demanding to know who was mucking about. These explosions were heard for several Sundays and the divers asked around with the local fishermen and coastguards, but no one seemed to know the cause. One theory was that the explosions were the work of divers demolishing the wreck of the "Brandenburg", a ship that had sunk after a mid-Channel collision. If this was right, it placed the source of the explosions about ten miles away and tied up with the distance estimate that Jess entered in the club records.

The second panic occurred one morning just after the inflatables had started out towards the buoy. There was a strong offshore breeze from the north and about six miles away they sighted two waterspouts. They looked like two wide and rather wobbly vertical jets of water, spinning and streaming up into a low and very turbulent cloud base. The spouts were moving at about six knots in a westerly direction and were roughing up the surface water very quickly.

The divers made it back to the beach at full throttle, just in case, but despite the very considerable mid-Channel wind sheer, the spouts maintained their direction and vanished when the cloud base seemed to reach down to the sea way past Dungeness. Local records showed that in the past there had been no reports of waterspouts so far east up-Channel.

The waterspouts must have been a portent of bad weather to come: during September it was impossible to make any dives at all, and at the end of the month a bad storm carried away the all-important wreck marker buoy. To relocate the 'plane would have taken the divers well into October, even if the weather had been favourable, so it was agreed that work for 1974 should stop and the project be re-examined with a view to further diving in early April, 1975.

The museum staff, by the end of 1974, had found themselves in the unusual position of organising a dig which they could influence little in terms of actual physical work. What made it even more unsatisfactory from their viewpoint was the fact that they could not see how much work had been done on the Me 109. Not unnaturally, they spent a great deal of time trying to estimate when the wreck would be ready for beaching, and went to a great deal of trouble to find a suitable beaching site. Jess had told them that the sand and clay could be dug away from beneath the aircraft in time, but what was urgently needed was some sort of mechanical underwater digging device to speed things up if they wanted the aircraft beached by the end of September, 1975. Jess had also told them that the aircraft appeared to be complete

40

as the divers had been able to feel all round the outline, and the digging had now gone all round the profile to a depth of about 6 inches leaving 5 feet to go. A small portion of wing surface had also been uncovered revealing a surface that was honeycombed with holes caused by corrosion, and very heavily encrusted with small clam shells. The divers had also brought up the right-hand wing radiator for examination. This proved to be a valuable find for the museum, as examination showed that the cooling area had been struck several times by small calibre bullets which were thought to be still in the radiator core.

By this stage in the dig, the museum staff had obtained formal ownership of the wreck. The local Receiver of Wrecks at Dover had been contacted and the salvage form described the remains as that of a single-seat fighter aircraft 1939–1945 era, Location OS.173. 13742/30431. The date of the find had been recorded as 26.5.74, and the existing owner the MoD S4c (Air).

The Ministry of Defence for their part had confirmed that "They no longer wished to retain an interest in the aircraft parts located by the Ashford & Tenterden Recovery Group, off Hythe . . . and had no objection to their recovery and retention by the Brenzett Aeronautical Museum." In true Civil Service style, the letter concluded with a disclaimer – ". . . must add that in no circumstances would this Ministry accept liability for any legal consequences arising from the activities of the recovery group, e.g. injury to persons, or damage to property" – which was fair enough.

On the vexed question of how to bring ashore a salvaged wartime aircraft, the museum staff considered several suitable beaching places. Dover Harbour had ideal facilities for beaching a wreck, so a letter was dispatched to the Harbour Master. The Harbour Master regretfully declined the privilege of handling the wreck on the grounds that he didn't really fancy the chance of towing a "possibly loaded Me 109" through the main shipping area. "The cross-Channel boats must not be delayed," he said, quite rightly. So Dover was out of the running. The concrete slipway at Hythe had its attractions. It was local to the operation. It also had a steep twenty foot drop going in, so Hythe was out.

The Redoubt at Dymchurch had a splendid beaching area

with sand and shingle beaches. The concrete promenade wall was ideal for mounting of cranes and lorries with winches, and there was also a private road connecting with the coast road for all transport. Further investigation showed that the area belonged to the Southern Water Authority, who were kind enough to grant permission to the museum for the beaching. A Mr Wightwick, who was in charge of the Redoubt for the SWA, began to take an interest in the project and, as a special privilege, let the museum staff use the private area and allowed them to lock the gate to keep the curious out – a special blessing during the holiday season.

Having established just where they were going to bring the aircraft ashore, the museum staff considered the next priority, which was where to take the aircraft for stripping and cleaning before it became an exhibit at the museum. As David Buchanan put it, "At that time we just didn't know how much of an aircraft there was to salvage, and farmers with barns to let do tend to get rather specific about area. He went on, "Farmers not unnaturally, also like to know just when a 'let' is to commence, and we were rather vague about this. 'As soon as the divers can dig it up' was usually considered too speculative by prospective landlords."

Although diving had stopped for the winter and spring, Jess found that more of his time was being taken up in a search for a suitable digging device. Meetings had been arranged with local plant and machinery firms with a view to looking over the specialist tools available. In fact, there were no suitable designs at all on the local market. As one plant salesman put it, "We don't often get asked for a digger that will shift blue clay whilst working in forty feet of very salt water." The fact that the digger claws had to be super sensitive and not damage anything it touched, whilst the controller worked in a maximum of four feet of visibility and a minimum of total darkness, had also tended to complicate the specification.

A possible solution to the digging problem was offered by two visitors to one of the museum's digs. The visitors came from Bournemouth and were both in Kent in search of old aircraft parts. Not unnaturally, they had been passed on to David Buchanan as the local authority on World War Two aircraft, and a friendship had sprung up over the years. The visitors, Bill Hamblin and Peter Foote, were both considered experts in the restoration of vintage aircraft, Bill currently working on a wartime Harvard and an Auster 5, and Peter having a nearly complete Me 109.

The magic formula for fast underwater digging was high pressure water. This they generously offered to supply by means of a Coventry Climax fire pump for the divers. Jess was dubious about the claims made for the pump. He was also unsure of the exact dimensions of the pump and felt that it would not be easy getting it onto the inflatable and out to the wreck. He also doubted that it would be able to shift the clinging blue clay in the quantities needed to free the Me 109 by the end of 1975. Bill and Peter stuck to their claims and promised to bring the fire pump up from Bournemouth as soon as the divers restarted work in April, 1975.

A second idea for digging was also under discussion – a kind of underwater vacuum cleaner which would push compressed air into the sand and blow it away from the site. Such a device would also have the merit of being able to blow out the areas previously cleared by the divers which automatically silted up again each week. Eventually it was found that insufficient air pressure was available to move the blue clay without having to hand dig it first, so that idea was scrapped.

Diving commenced for the 1975 season later than expected owing to the poor weather. Alan Griggs was sent out first to drop a buoy in the approximate location of the wreck, and the divers started a boat search using grappling hooks and weighted lines stretched between the boats. It was June 7 before the wreck had been relocated and the divers made a close inspection of the wreck site, clearing accumulated winter debris and checking the aircraft for any evidence of corrosion spread. Naturally, all the digging done the previous year had silted up, but this proved quite easy to clear away again. On the weekend of the 14/15 June, the divers and the museum team started to work jointly on the preparation of the landing site at the Redoubt for the anticipated beaching of the aircraft later in the season.

The Bournemouth Group, Bill Hambling and Peter Foote, now country members of the Museum Group, arrived with the Coventry Climax water pump and a clinker bottomed

43

row-boat on a trailer. The Bournemouth boys apologised for the condition of the row-boat and Graham (B) said he wouldn't have got into it without the water pump. After some argument, the divers put the clinker boat in the water, the trailer with the water pump was brought down to the water edge and, by dint of much combined manhandling, the water pump was lowered into the boat and the water level came up to within two inches of the top of the hull.

Obviously this was an unacceptable risk. The whole platform was too unstable for any form of sea operation. Overcoming his naturally suspicious nature, Graham (B) suggested that, having got the thing in the boat and on the water, why not give the pump a trial run. After a swing or two the pump started and the inlet pipe started sucking up water at a great rate.

Graham took the outlet pipe about two feet away and pushed the force nozzle into the sand in about three feet of water. The miracle happened just as the Bournemouth team had suggested, and the force nozzle pushed its way down into the sand. They now had their digging tool.

Jess said, "We shall just have to fit the pump into one of the inflatables, and it's not going to be mine." This decision sounded rather harsh, but it was based on sound common sense as Jess had the largest boat and could carry up to six divers. Eventually Derek offered his inflatable and the Bournemouth team put a special reinforced bottom and mounting to accommodate the water pump in the boat. Graham (B) lent his outboard engine for the trials. It was thought that the pump boat would be better served with a regular operator and Graham (L) seemed to be the best of the divers in swinging rapid life into the engine of the Coventry Climax, so he was elected by everyone as pump-boss for the operation.

The sea trials of the Coventry Climax inflatable were interesting, in that no one quite knew what would happen. A large mass was now placed roughly central to the boat and Graham (L) took the craft away with due caution about how much water it was going to ship. Inflatables are virtually unsinkable, but they can be capsized and the normal righting drill certainly wouldn't work with the Coventry Climax inverted under water. Rather to the surprise of all, it was found that the inflatable didn't ship water and it planed quite

44

steadily. If Graham opened the throttle too quickly, the bows would start to lift, necessitating him to run briskly to the front to bring the bows down. A really large wave would almost certainly have capsized the craft, so the divers decided to stick to the convoy system in case Graham needed rescuing. After a time he got very skilled at keeping the bows at the right level and began to start steering into the wash of the other boats to get the boat up on the step and to start planing like a speedboat. The other divers sat tight in their inflatables waiting for Graham to fall in, but didn't have any luck. The suspicion gradually began to dawn on some of them that either Graham was exhibiting great skill in boat control, or he was making it look much more dangerous than it really was. There were no volunteers to take over in his place, however.

Once out at the marker buoy, a new drill had to be established to make the best use of the underwater time. The water pump proved to be a fantastic improvement over hand digging. The main problem was that the diver using the nozzle had to anchor himself firmly on to the wreck or the force would simply blow him away from the wreck site. Normally there would be two divers down at a time. This usually left two in the inflatable keeping the logs and operating the Coventry Climax. If other divers came along from the club, a rota would be worked out and some hand digging attempted at the same time to help quicken the work rate.

Progress was such that both wing surfaces were cleared together with a generous area of the underside of the aircraft right down to the tail plane.

Using the force pump, it was at last possible to start digging down towards the unseen parts of the aircraft. Being upside-down, the most important area was that of the cockpit, and about four feet of spoil had to be removed all round in order to bring the sea bed level to the necessary depth. Naturally, when the sand and clay had been blown away, water took its place but the divers found they were able to grope around the dark pools and feel, rather than see, what had been hidden under the sea for 35 years. Visibility was so poor on occasions that the divers began to experience the phosphorescent lighting of the tiny marine life.

Hand and visual examination of the 'plane showed that

the wing leading edge slots were locked in the open position. The landing flaps were still attached to the wings, but could be moved by hand. They were still in the closed position when uncovered. Although the undercarriage struts were locked firmly in the open position, the U/C fairings had been stripped off the legs and no trace of the metal parts was found around the wreck site. Digging was still going on around the area of the cockpit, but it was obvious that the pilots' canopy, front screen and rear canopy had all vanished. Jess had maintained all along that the cockpit was unoccupied, and this in fact proved to be right. There was one moment of panic when one of the divers felt what he thought to be a human skull in the cockpit. Closer examination proved the object to be the base of an oxygen bottle, and the divers probably felt rather relieved that their work would not involve the removal and reinterment of a body after all this time.

5 FINAL EXCAVATION AND LIFT

During the summer, a number of changes were evident to Jess, both in his diving crews and in the approach to the underwater dig. The basic team of four divers continued unchanged – Jess, both Grahams and Derek – but other members who had started on the project had either lost interest or found it all too much like hard work. It was very hard physical work, and the crew were often at sea for six hours, with diving shifts of 20–70 minutes, depending on whether the diver was digging or watching. Those digging naturally used up their air supply much faster. Underwater, usually the only sound the diver would hear would be the passage of his own air bubbles.

In an effort to speed things up, Graham (L) and Jess took a week off work. Jess was down, working on the aircraft when he heard the sound of a boat approaching the site. Naturally Jess waited for Graham to signal the boat away with the diving flag, but the noise got steadily nearer and sounded like a trawler. Having no wish to be caught up in a net, Jess surfaced, expecting to see the boat within 50 yards of the inflatable. In fact it was still over half a mile away. Underwater sound always confuses the diver, even the expert.

Eventually shoals of small crabs living on the wreck got fed up with the divers and died off in their masses. The crabs were immediately replaced by whelks, who really surrounded the site, providing the divers with the only diversion they had from digging. The death of the crabs seemed to have been from natural causes, not from underwater pollution. Being near the power station at Dungeness, a very close watch was kept for underwater contamination, and Jess said that if there had been a seepage, the divers would have read about it in the papers between their weekend-only jaunts.

Another diver, Michael Henderson, joined the diving team. He was not related to Jess and in fact came from the Dover Sub Aqua Club, with a wide experience of different diving conditions, from the North Foreland area to places like the Seychelles and Cornwall, diving on a Roman Galleon at 180 feet. Visibility there was fabulous, but because everything was so easy, you could get lulled into a sense of false security. He said that putting his hand on a lion fish, which has a sting rather like a scorpion, brought his mind back to underwater danger very sharply. For Michael, working on the Me 109 at Hythe became a challenge. He had no interest in the aircraft and was quite happy at the future thought of handing it over to the museum.

The Me 109 meant working underwater just by feel which gave him a unique diving experience that would stand him in good stead for diving almost anywhere in the world. That was his motivation for staying with the Hythe team. The diving gave him a "buzz"; it was always absorbing, concentrating the mind on one objective only. A totally different dimension from any other form of sport.

With the passing of time, the divers found that their approach to the work began to change as experience showed them how corners could be cut. When using the pump, they discovered that it was better diving on a fast tide, as this helped to clear the silt away from the site. A number of special signals were worked out using the line to the pump operator from underwater. The pump code became: one pull for start, two pulls to stop pump, three for more power, and a series of continuous pulls if the diver got into difficulties. This system worked well, unless the pump operator got bored with sitting in the inflatable with nothing to look at except sea. Evil minded pump operators had been known to gently increase the pressure to the diver's force nozzle. Being unprepared, the diver would suddenly find that he was moving more soil than usual. Naturally the equal and opposite effect of the extra energy also pressed harder on the diver, and usually ended with his handhold slipping and the diver moving further and further away from the worksite in the vanishing visibility. Frantic pulls on the pump line would restore the status quo, while the diver wandered around in a mist of swirling particles trying to find the aircraft again. Jess said that such moments were frustrating, because they had no sound communication with the inflatables and by the time your underwater shift had finished, tempers had generally settled down again.

The divers always worked as a team right from the start of the day when boat loading commenced. Graham (B), however, prided himself on his independence and when he arrived first one morning he decided to unhook his trailer and inflatable single-handed and run it down to the beach. He started off down the ramp in front of the trailer and was surprised to find it overtaking him. To keep it under control you normally have to zig-zag, but the trailer took over. Graham said he sat on it at first, but had to dive off when it hit the rocks at the bottom and bounced over to dive in, nose first.

When the other divers arrived, they said that Graham seemed quite casual about the way he managed without their help, until someone noticed the tyre tracks.

As the oldest diver, actually admitting to 47 years, Graham usually contrived to get the most out of any departure from the normal routine. He was a most reliable diving buddy, but somehow, when separated from the vulgar herd, he usually contrived to get involved in unexpected circumstances. On one launch from Hythe, a rather heavy sea mist had made it obvious that the army would not be operating the firing range. Instead of taking the flotilla of inflatables out on the usual dog-leg course to avoid the range, Jess had led the much shorter way to the diving buoy in a straight line across the range.

48

Graham (B), being lumbered with the Coventry Climax in his boat, followed behind at a rather slower pace. The others had been waiting at the marker buoy for about ten minutes when the sea mist suddenly cleared. The army, who had obviously been waiting for just that moment, opened up on the sea targets with small arms fire. The divers could distinctly hear the plop-plopping of bullets hitting the water. In front of the bullet splashes, the pump boat could be seen going at full throttle, bows out of the water, with delicate feathers of spray rising from each side of the boat. On joining the boats on the marker buoy, Graham's face was said to have the look of a man who wandered absent mindedly through the gun fight at the OK Corral and got away with it. Curiously, on this occasion, the range boat didn't put in its usual rapid appearance to warn the divers that firing was to commence.

Someone suggested that it was the range boat crews who were doing the firing and they would certainly get Graham on the way back.

Towards the end of August, progress on the digging was so good that the museum group were cautioned to expect an attempt at a lift by September. The group had been hard at work modifying old oil drums of 45 gallon capacity to act as air bags for lift. The drums had to be fitted with circular wire strops at one end and filled with enough water to make them slightly buoyant. The idea was to place them at carefully selected lift points on the aircraft and blow the water out with compressed air so that the whole 'plane would lift up and be capable of towing by trawler toward the Redoubt.

Peter Foote and Bill Hamlyn from Bournemouth had commenced the construction of a beaching trolley. This ingenious device had to be "tailor made" to fit onto the aircraft when it reached a suitable depth of water at the Redoubt. It was proposed that the trolley would take all the body stresses of a badly weakened airframe and could be winched up the beach onto the promenade.

The centre breakwaters at the Redoubt were all marked with yellow polythene buoys on every fourth groyne down to low water mark, and, although the beach in-between was pretty clear of obstructions, museum staff and divers, together with families and friends, worked very hard removing rocks and other marine flotsam from the area so that the beaching trolley would have a clear passage up the beach.

Excitement was running high that a lift could take place given another two weeks of fine weather. The divers tried to get a line down under the engine with a view to anchoring it to the undercarriage to help take the lifting stresses, but the weather broke before this could be completed. Once again, diving had to be abandoned for 1975. Just to rub in the unlucky element, the wreck marker buoy disappeared during October.

Naturally there was a strong sense of anti-climax at this set-back. No one could predict what damage the storms could do to the aircraft now that it was dug out of its protective shell of clay. The divers had started on a plan to plant out an underwater slatted wooden fence to protect the underwater site, but the weather was too bad to permit any last minute attempts to put this scheme into operation.

Having made the decision to wait, it would have been understandable if members had given up at this point. In fact, Jess said that those involved kept up the regular Friday 'phone-in, just in case conditions improved to allow some winter diving. To Jess, the whole project by this time had become almost an obsession, certainly a personal challenge, and he would often go out on the winter evenings, staring out to sea in the direction of the wreck trying to develop new methods of speeding up the work in the spring. Naturally the sub-aqua club continued its training of new and younger members, who were generally beginning to feel that they had been left out of things. Jess had been diving officer at the club up to this time and, being honest with himself, he felt that he should resign the position, as the salvage prevented him from giving members his full help. A new club leader was appointed to allow the continuation of work. In view of the dangers of the underwater work, it was felt that new members should not take on work on the aircraft.

The museum undertook to give the Coventry Climax a major overhaul during the winter. When the divers started using it, it was in poor mechanical condition and leaked like a sieve at first. It also had to have an oil change after each pumping session and the old oil began to look like milk, so Jess was naturally worried that they might be doing some irreparable damage.

The winter was also a good time to get the maintenance done on the diving gear. Normally each diver looks after his gear personally, and takes a great deal of pride in the effort. The volume of work undertaken by the club had naturally been considerably higher than usual over the last two years, so special attention had to be given to the condition of the air bottles. Little corrosion forms in aluminium bottles, but steel bottles tend to corrode and silica gels are used to contain the iron oxide. The air used in the bottles has to be filtered three times to remove first the water, then the oil and, finally, the dust. This action keeps the bottles fairly clean. Special attention was also paid to the condition of the wet suits and to the bottle valve gear. Tubes and hoses can split or suffer general deterioration and have to be replaced immediately when these conditions show. Pressure gauges have to be checked for accuracy and any sign of misting on the glass means immediate replacement. Even at the shallow depth the divers were working, an unexpected loss of air could mean the life of a diver if he could not surface immediately.

Diving recommenced in April, 1976 and by May 9 a weighted line drawn between two inflatables had snagged on the aircraft and the divers were back in business.

This year they were joined by Jim Reed from the Cambridge sub-aqua group. His diving experience was over eight years and included dives in Italian waters. His first impressions on diving on the aircraft with the Hythe group were that conditions were more hostile. It was colder at the start of the season and the problem of working in almost nil visibility was new to him. He was surprised to find that the seabed seemed to be only muddy sand without rocks and that the examination of the wreck was to be by touch alone. On his later dives the visibility improved somewhat to about four feet and, like the other divers, he had found himself astonished at the lack of damage and corrosion to the aircraft. In fact, his first dive at Hythe had been in April and he had been given a 60-foot search line and an opportunity to help relocate the aircraft. He said that his briefing from Jess was simple: "The buoy dropped by Alan Griggs is approximately where we were working last September. Go down the buoy line and attach your search line to the anchor at the bottom. Fin out to the full extent of your line and then wade a complete circle. If the line catches on anything, it will almost certainly be the aircraft. Then fin to the snag, fasten your line to the undercarriage, go back to the buoy line, anchor and reposition it securely to the aircraft, then surface up the buoy line to the inflatable."

Jim said that, as they sat in the inflatable 1½ miles from shore, there was nothing except the buoy marker to indicate that there might be an aircraft forty feet below them. He pushed himself off backwards from the inflatable, one hand gripping the buoy line. There was a four knot current trying to tug him away and he felt that it would be hard work trying to swim back if he lost his handhold. He went down the line head first, hand over hand, finning hard, and by the time he was half way down the visibility had dropped quickly, and the water looked dark grey. As he neared the bottom, visibility was almost two feet and he held up one hand in front of his head, trying to feel for the seabed. Pulling on the line took him to the anchor weight and he paused here to try to get his bearings. Apart from the anchor and a little muddy sand, there was almost nothing else that could be seen. No fish, no seaweed, his only company the sound of the bubbles of his exhaled air.

He carefully fastened his search line to the anchor and, using the tidal drift, floated away from the anchor until the sixty feet of thin nylon rope was fully used, and left his body streaming flagwise in the four knot pull.

By using the current, he had now established a geometric radius to the circle of search. His body weight made him slightly heavy and he commenced a part swim, part walk, around the circumference of a 120-foot circle, keeping the line taut. He remembered that Jess had said that the Messerschmitt undercarriage reached upward about four feet from the sea bed and that, if he had dived in the right place, the search line would catch. The trick was to know when he had completed the circle. Had the line snagged, it would have become greatly foreshortened, but this did not happen. He continued to move around until the tidal drift seemed identical to the start of his search, trying to move him from the anchor with maximum force. This low visibility was different: it was all feeling, the redevelopment of forgotten senses. When he was sure that he had completed more than the prescribed circle, he commenced the recoiling of the search line, finning his way carefully back to the anchor.

Examination of his watch told him that he had been under-water for twenty-four minutes. He untied the end of the search rope and commenced the ascent up the marker buoy line. As visibility improved, he looked around for the boat bottom. It was, unexpectedly, to his right, with the line going up in a great curve to compensate for the drift. When he broke surface, he established a handhold and then passed his weight belt and then his body pack to the waiting divers.

By dint of finning down and pulling up with his hands, he wriggled aboard the inflatable. He shook his head at Jess and said, "It's a bit different – diving at Hythe." He felt very cold and rather frustrated.

It was May before the divers found the aircraft again, using a weighted line drawn between two inflatables. Jess dived first. He said he was sure it was the aircraft and pre-sently gave the agreed signal of three pulls on the line to confirm the news. The other divers had all seen the wreck before and it was rather cold, so there was no mad rush to go down. Jim was curious and went down next. He said there was an awful lot of line out and it seemed to take a long time before he arrived at the seabed. Visibility was almost six feet on this dive and Jim found that Jess was waiting to give him a tour of the aircraft in the grand manner. He felt very im-pressed, seeing the aircraft for the first time, and was sur-prised to see that the undercarriage oleo struts were shining like new chrome plating. There were no wheels, just stub axles, and the U/C fairings had vanished. Jess said that very little of the sand and clay removed the previous year had returned, and it was possible now to look right across toward each wing tip. One large painted black cross was clearly visible.

Together the two divers finned right round the aircraft looking for special features and possible storm damage. The engine and bearers appeared intact, the underbelly bomb rack looked solid, but the fuselage skin seemed rather pliable to the touch. On the leading edges of the starboard wing, Jess pointed out the gun ports and through areas of corroded skin it was possible to see the MG 17 guns and ammunition belts, still in place. Most of the wing surface was corroded with small holes and encrusted with tiny shells and other marine life. The wing slats were locked out and did not move to the touch, but the wing flaps were closed and could be rotated upward by hand. The tiny square wing tips appeared to have rotted somewhat, but the navigation lights and bits of wiring were visible. When the divers followed the fuselage to the rear, it was obvious that the tailplane was still in position, although one of the external bracing struts seemed loose in its attachment socket and the tail wheel and oleo were missing. The control surfaces on the tail appeared to have been fabric covered and some of this had been torn, exposing a painted, friable fabric. It was impossible to look into the cockpit so, using touch alone, hand inspection suggested that the dash panel had vanished and one or two instruments hung down on lengths of wire harness. The control column was still inside, but looked fragile. Jess had looked for evidence of hits by cannon or MG fire, but he could only find holes clearly made by the action of corrosion. As Jim remarked afterwards, it certainly seemed that they had uncovered an almost complete aircraft. After this condition report to the museum, hopes of beaching a good specimen of the Messerschmitt clan began to rise.

Good progress was made with the final site clearing during June. One incident did occur, but the divers all seemed rather vague about the actual date. Big Graham couldn't make it that weekend, so Jess borrowed his inflatable and handed over the piloting thereof to a very experienced diver from another club. For some strange reason, none of the divers seemed to be able to remember his name. Jess said, "Well, I briefed him how to take the pump boat out and, because it was slower, to make his own way to the marker, mind the firing range – all the local facts – but I wasn't at all worried about him as he had been using inflatables for years and knew the local area. Unfortunately he did omit to tell me one important detail, and that was that with the passing of time he had become very shortsighted. Naturally, that wouldn't have mattered, but on this trip he forgot his glasses and didn't discover the fact until he was a long way out to sea. We followed him out about ten minutes later and, when we got to the buoy, there was absolutely no sign of him. We waited about half an hour whilst the divers got into their gear, but still there was no sign of him. Everything was ready to start work, but we didn't have the pump and, after a bit longer, I began to feel a bit evil about the situation. My first thoughts were that he had mishandled the boat, capsizing it, and had gone missing. At that distance from the shore, he probably hadn't been spotted.

"I took my boat ashore, followed by the others, and got hold of the local coastguard and explained the problem. These coastguards really spring into action if they think there is danger and in no time at all they had organised a helicopter, in case our missing diver had had an engine breakdown and was drifting off down Channel. We actually had to load our boats onto our trailers to move further East along the coast toward Sandgate. This would enable us to save half an hour in case he had broken down and was drifting East. When I drove up the slope and looked back, I saw a tiny dot on the horizon – and it was him, quite safe and complaining bitterly that we had all missed the rendezvous. In fact, he had passed the marker buoy without spotting it and gone out to sea for over five miles before the thought struck him that something was wrong.

"Naturally, the next thing to do was to get back and cancel the search and apologise to all concerned. Those choppers cost about £100 an hour to operate. On the way back to shore, I gave him a bit of a dressing down; it wasn't that we weren't glad to see him, but I had been mentally rehearsing a short speech to Graham (B) about how sorry we were to lose £500's worth of inflatable that we had borrowed, not to mention the Coventry Climax pump.

"When the boats were all back ashore, the law arrived, attracted, no doubt, by the helicopter movement. Having taken all our particulars, he decided that it was time the club had a boat-to-boat inspection of its safety equipment. Fortunately it was all in its proper place and in working order. Meanwhile this poor bloke who had caused all the trouble because he forgot his glasses was standing by, hoping that it was just a private nightmare and that he would awaken in the bar of the 'Swan', holding a pint. The coastguards, however, took a very generous view of the whole business, saying that they would rather have ten false alarms than have an incident go unreported."

During July the divers got a rope under the engine and braced to the undercarriage, and also fitted the lifting rings. A convoy set off on July 3 with two inflatables loaded up with five lift drums each, another inflatable with twelve air bottles and equipment for five divers, and two speedboats loaded up with divers. The whole thing took on the air of a combined operations exercise. Holidaymakers were all very intrigued with this action and rumours began to pass around the coast that something was up. The plan was to fit and fully inflate nine drums to the undercarriage in preparation to lifting the 'plane the following weekend.

To get the drums underwater, a pulley was attached to the undercarriage lifting ring with a continuous rope going round another pulley and buoy on the surface. Drums were attached to the rope, one at a time, then flooded so that they could be pulled down straight to the waiting divers. The divers then fitted each drum to a lifting ring and blew out its water content, using the octopus rigs on their demand valves. This part of the operation worked like a precision drill, and nine drums were fitted and blown in about twenty minutes. Each drum gave about 450 lbs lift when full of air, so with nine drums in position there was something over 4,000 lbs of lift straining at the aircraft.

There were three divers underwater at the moment one of the lifting clamps broke, starting off an interesting sequence of events. The second clamp got the full effect of the lift transfer and this also broke, releasing all nine drums at once. These took off in an upward direction, rather like Polaris missiles, and ascended past the inflatable to heights reportedly varying from five to fifty feet. Having equalised their internal pressures, the nine drums then returned back to the water, the waves rapidly dispersing them away from the diving area. Amazingly, no one was killed. It could, at its worst, have damaged or even sunk some of the little flotilla of boats. Certainly those underwater were lucky not to have suffered injury and those on the surface could have been hit by falling drums.

When the underwater disturbance had cleared and the divers checked for injury, they surfaced thoughtfully to see how their surface team had fared.

The Messerschmitt, placidly unmoved on the sea bed, appeared to be making an unmistakable Churchillian gesture with its undercarriage.

6 THE BEACHING

During the weekend of July 10/11, the damaged lifting clamps were replaced with a heavy chain. The divers managed to fit twenty drums to both the engine and the undercarriage. On this occasion they were only partly filled with air and everything remained firmly in position.

Fisherman Alan Griggs was brought back into action for the weekend of July 18/19. The "Joan of Arc" had been replaced with a new boat the "Opportunity", the previous summer. This was exactly the boat he had been visualising for his work when he accidentally discovered the Me 109 in 1974 – ten feet longer, a more powerful engine and the Decca navigator. For insurance purposes, he now had a £60,000 boat to go trawling daily. The self-made fisherman had arrived at the next measure of his luck.

The divers spent the morning of the Saturday working in pairs to clear away as much of the remaining silt and mud as possible. By 1.30 p.m. the "Opportunity" arrived at the site and took aboard a portable compressor, together with an airline. Two of the divers took the airline down and work was started on blowing the remainder of the air from the lift drums. In spite of having a stable platform for the compressor, the divers began to complain that much of the compressed air was failing to reach the drums. This was partly due to the airline leaking underwater and partly because the work seemed to be too hard for the compressor. The divers simply ran out of lift air before all the drums were blown. Time was getting on and, after a short discussion the divers decided that it might be worth getting a line from the 'plane onto the winch on the trawler deck, just to see if a gentle pull could get the aircraft moving out of the sand. The divers standing by on the sea bed were gratified to watch the aircraft slowly moving along out of the mud, for the first time in thirty-six years. After a fifty yard tow, it was obvious that the aircraft did not have enough buoyancy to lift, and to prevent damage it was allowed to settle on the seabed for the night. Alan said that it felt very heavy at the other end of the tow line and he found it difficult to steer in any but a series of wide S bends.

The museum staff made some modifications to the faulty compressor and added an extra unit to boost the volume of air passed down the airline. A new hose was also fitted to cure possible leaks and a new angled lance was fitted to get the air into the drums. Output from both compressors now shared a single air line. Both compressors were securely anchored to the deck of the "Opportunity", as the old single unit had been prone to move about on the deck when running.

These modifications were all completed by midnight on the Saturday.

The following morning, with the same order of battle, the compressors were again coaxed reluctantly into life and work commenced on blowing the lift drums. Alan had taken the precaution of mounting an improvised towing tackle, consisting of a tow block with a roller that allowed the tow line to move from one side of the stern to the other without affecting the steering too much. Underwater, Jess and Michael had a team operation going on as Graham (L) sent down the water-filled drums. Michael unclipped them and passed them over to Jess, who in turn attached them to the correct lifting point and then started to blow out the remaining air. Things were going so well that the aircraft slowly became light and, almost imperceptibly, started to lift.

Visibility, as usual, was poor and the divers couldn't really see what was happening till Jess discovered that he was having to reach up to attach the drums. Michael said he turned round to get another drum off the line and, when he turned back, the 'plane had gone, and he just had a glimpse of Jess's fins disappearing above his head. With commendable forethought, Michael decided to surface, in case the wreck got temperamental and came down on top of him. There was some confusion as to what happened next. Alan got a signal to start towing from Jess, who had now reached the surface. From

Alan's viewpoint, he knew he wanted all the power he had and he opened the throttles wide.

Michael, coming up in poor visibility, probably passed the tail end of the Messerschmitt going down, undoubtedly still full of sand. Relieved of this 3,000 lbs of weight, Alan probably found that the tow started to go faster than expected, snaking about behind but invisible from the deck, as the aircraft didn't rise all the way to the surface. The areodynamics of a fully slotted and inverted aircraft, wings with one flap up and another down and no aft balance, must have made for interesting steering.

Jess and Michael had discovered the loss of part of the tail by this time and were waving madly to Alan to get him to stop the tow. As he could not hear what they were shouting, he naturally assumed that they were making encouraging noises, so he continued the tow at full throttle. Perhaps fortunately, the tide level had dropped a bit and the aircraft grounded about half a mile from shore, slap in one corner of the Hythe firing range.

The divers re-formed over the new resting place and hastily put down a marker buoy before commencing an underwater inspection for damage.

This must have proved the biggest disappointment of all. About a third of the rear fuselage was no longer attached and, worse still, both engine bearers had fractured, allowing the whole engine to tilt up so that the airscrew blades were now passing through the centre of the lifting straps and, rocking gently in the tidal flow, were busily sawing through the webbing. Immediate salvage on the straps recommenced underwater, with the inflatable and the "Opportunity" standing back just in case. The divers' speed in renewing the straps was just that bit slower than the sawing action of the airscrew blades and, in no time at all, the lift drums were disappearing upward again, doing the "Polaris" trick. Alan, fearing a change in "fisherman's luck", proceeded to stand off the site sharply, as he had no wish to see an oil drum coming up through the bottom of his new boat. The divers abandoned the underwater race and got back in their boats. Michael said that the next part was the worst: the recovery of the lift drums, which the wind and the tide were now dispersing over a wide area of sea. When you got the inflatable alongside a drum, it had about twenty gallons of sea water inside which had to be emptied out before the drum could be lifted aboard. It was rather like a large scale "apple bobbing" contest, with divers, drums and boats scattered in all directions down Channel. Eventually all the drums were secured, and the divers were just re-forming and thinking of a well-earned pint or two ashore when the range boat arrived to warn them that they were in the firing range and the troops would start firing very shortly.

By mutual arrangement, the divers and the museum staff agreed to try to beach the aircraft on Saturday, 24 July. There was no problem with the fantastic summer weather and the museum team assembled at the Redoubt to check that the marker buoys were all in position, and that the lorries, winch and recovery gear were all ready. The divers arrived in strength at the marker buoy and, as soon as work started, out popped the range boat to tell them that firing was about to commence and to get the hell out of it. This nearly started World War 3 for a moment as far as the divers were concerned, but eventually hard talking and reason prevailed. It was agreed that the army should get on with their firing practice and the divers would go out again during the lunch break and muffle the propeller blades with sacking. The army took the rest of the day at firing practice and would start their Sunday practice an hour later, thus giving the divers the benefit of a 10.45 a.m. high tide.

The muffling was duly completed in the time and fresh plans were made for an early start on the Sunday morning.

Alan Griggs' boat was first on the marker buoy on Sunday. He carried the all-important lift drums, a large complement of divers, David Buchanan from the museum and two extra divers up from Somerset from the Wells Diving Group. All the other divers brought out the inflatables from shore and the work of fitting the lift drums started. Jess and Jim dived first and fitted six drums, then Michael and Graham (B) put on another six. Graham (L) remained on the boat sending the drums down the line to the aircraft faster than the divers could take them off to blow and fix and, in half an hour, fifteen drums had been fitted and the aircraft started to lift again. Jess said the situation underwater began to get a little confused, as all the divers wanted to go down and watch

60

what was happening. Eventually there were about twelve of them going up and down like yo-yos, and they were beginning to get in each other's way. To get things organised again, Jess ordered all the spare divers up. Two of them went off with Michael to see if they could find the tail and put a buoy marker on it. They found the old manhole cover they had used as an anchor, but, before they could complete the marking, they found they were running short of air and had to surface. Jess was now back on his inflatable and Alan took up the tow, and the little fleet of boats started off for the entrance to the Redoubt buoy marking lane.

On shore at the Redoubt, the museum team were getting short-wave radio progress reports from David. Peter Foote had been appointed beachmaster and was worrying about using the beaching trolley, because of the new damage to the aircraft and the structural imbalance. The problem had already been solved for him, as the tow from the firing range had to be started early since the army had already started firing across the range. The divers did not get a second opportunity to fit the trolley.

Bill Hamblin went out in one of the boats to meet the in-coming flotilla, swapping places with David Buchanan when he went ashore to be ahead of the winching operation. Bill said that they gave him the job of relaying the ship-to-shore messages with the radio telephone. This caused a panic or two as nobody told him how it worked and some rather odd messages started coming over the air till he got it sorted out.

Len Green, the man from the museum who had made the first identification of the Me 109 back in 1974, was sitting in one of the boats also with a radio link with David. To him, the moment was a very special one. After three years of talking to the divers, he had formed a firm mental impression of what they were going to see. The reports had been of the slow excavation of a complete aircraft, with some corrosion but all the main features more or less intact, even to the painted cross on the wing. The damage reports he had just heard had modified his impression considerably. Just what would come up on the end of the winch wire? Admittedly, so long as all of it came ashore one way or another, the museum staff were very experienced in the reassembly of damaged aircraft; but, after all that work, it would have been rather special to see a complete aircraft at the end of the tow . . .

The beachmaster was watching the approaching flotilla. The "Opportunity" must be getting into shallow water by now. He noticed that the tidal drift was across the entrance to the yellow tunnel of buoy markers. That drift could be a problem. Perhaps the divers could hold the wing tips when the tow stopped from the trawler.

He looked back at the beach behind him, noting that everyone was in position. His eyes took in the huge mobile army crane that dominated the sea wall. This had been a totally unexpected bonus. Some of the Royal Engineers had been doing a bridge building exercise nearby and had stopped to watch the excitement. A friendly word or two resulted in their offering the museum the use of the latest computerised mobile crane to lift the bits ashore. As an old hand at aircraft work, he had long ceased to be amazed at the way people wanted to help in recovery work. Human curiosity was a very strong force and seemed to have no boundaries relating to age, sex or occupation. Looking along the sea wall he saw that the crowd of onlookers had grown. At first, it had just been families and friends, but now two or three hundred people had appeared from nowhere. Looking back at the earth slope up behind the Redoubt, more people were gathering. Although he could not see the coast road behind the Redoubt, the main holiday traffic was slowing and cars turned into the side to disgorge families coming to see the excitement.* The police were already well in evidence along the sea wall, trying to keep the crowd back from the beaching area. A BBC camera unit was setting up shop, and most of the two teams' members had brought cameras and passed them to wives with detailed instructions of what pictures to take. In fact, there was a superfluity of cameras around, whose operators were about to learn that taking pictures out to sea in a bright haze of sunlight tended to produce pictures which would abound in silhouette rather than contrasting tonal values. The more experienced photographers made due allowance for this by giving a stop or two more than usual to compensate, or chose positions to the side of the beaching area to avoid photographing directly into the glare.

* *See Appendix*

Along the sloping ramp below the sea wall, the winching lorry had taken up a position with its back to the sea. The JCB, which was present to lift the aircraft clear of the sand in its massive scoop, was positioned parallel to the sea. Everything was as ready as it ever could be for the final act of salvage.

7 THE RELUCTANT MESSERSCHMITT

Aboard the "Opportunity", trawler skipper Alan had been finding fresh problems in the tow. The inverted leading edge of the aircraft presented such a large angle of attack to the direction of motion that an unexpected amount of lift was being generated. The engine was still hanging on by one unbroken bearer at a wide angle to the direction of motion, and conspired to make the steering a matter of some difficulty. Now, Alan's attention was diverted by the rising sea bed and his echo sounder was warning of a depth of only twelve feet.

The "Opportunity" drew six feet, and Alan had no intention of grounding his boat in what, in a few minutes, would be a falling tide. He lined the boat up on the beaching area for the last time, made the signal to the divers to cut the tow and then commenced a wide sweep to starboard away from the inflatables.

The aircraft slowed rapidly and David sent the radio signal to shore for the divers to bring out the winch line. Two of the diving boats took up positions alongside the wing-tips of the aircraft to try to keep it between the yellow buoy markers. To David, standing on the deck of the "Opportunity", it seemed a very long time before the tow line was connected to the tow rope on the aircraft. He remembered being surprised that the sand was still streaming from the wreckage, colouring the water muddy brown. He recalled the provisional estimate of the weight that the museum had made back in 1974: at 4,500 lbs they had been 'way out', Jess's estimate of treble that figure giving a more reliable forecast.

Big Graham had his problems connecting the tow rope, but finally the larger tow line was pulled out with a light connecting line and the beachmaster was able to signal the winch operator to start work. The tow went in a series of twenty yard spurts. Meanwhile, back on shore, the back wheels of the lorry had to be banked up with sand to hold it in position. With the aircraft about forty feet from the tide mark, the blades of the propeller snagged on the sea bed and, as a final gesture of defiance, the prop unit and reduction gearing parted company from the engine. A further ten feet nearer the shore, the underside of the aircraft grounded for the last time and the long wait for the tidal fall began.

As the water level descended the apron below the sea wall, the beach master reflected on the next move. As yet, he didn't know that the propeller unit had come adrift. There was nothing to be seen except the tow rope entering the water and, a little further out, a pool of oily, muddy sea water on an otherwise unblemished surface. He decided that the crane on the sea wall should be connected next, the lifting points on the aircraft made secure by the divers, who were still working partly under water. This done, he signalled the crane driver to raise the crane jib ready for the final hoist and £60,000 of expensive army equipment pulsated into life, the giant jib slowly swinging upward toward the near vertical position. At an angle of 75° it stopped moving. The crowd went silent, expecting the first visual revelation. After a moment they heard the voice of the crane driver, plainly unable to believe his luck: "The bloody thing's stuck!" In fact it was two hours before the human will was re-imposed upon this computerised mechanical wonder, which was exhibiting signs of a nervous breakdown.

During the delay, the tide receded rapidly, revealing what first appeared to be the well-known Churchillian gesture by the legs of the undercarriage. Graham (B) remembered, thinking "God! How many times I've seen *that* these last three years!"

Without the wheels, the little stub axles looked rather naked, but despite thirty-six years of immersion, the oleo legs had retained their chromium plated shine.

In theory, the engine and bottom fuselage line with bomb rack and upper propeller blade should have been visible next.

In practice, it was the bomb rack and the undersurface of the two wings that appeared. The undercarriage retraction bays were clearly outlined. The U/C fairings which should have been attached to the U/C legs were not in evidence either, and David Buchanan, who had now regained the safety of the sea shore, began to make rapid mental notes about the missing pieces of airframe. As the water receded, the full undersides of port and starboard wings became visible, revealing the wing slots locked in the "out" position. To confirm the nationality of the aircraft, one black cross on a white ground could be clearly seen on the wing panelling. Back on the sea wall, the cross was also visible to the watching crowd, causing voices to rise, fingers to be pointed, arms waved vigorously and camera shutters whirred and clicked.

The black cross also seemed to produce strong emotions in one or two of the watchers. One large, middle-aged blonde woman seemed to suffer an immediate personality change, her voice going from affected to pure cockney at the drop of a swastika. She shared her experiences with all who would listen: ex-ATS, ex-predictor operator in AckAck command, unaided she had laid the gunsights that had terminated this Me 109's last sortie. One elderly gentleman moved away from the sound barrage muttering, "She must have had her best experiences laying in gunsites." Despite a police warning two other ladies, dressed in summer print dresses, started to wade in waist high to get a closer look at the Me. The oily mess floating on the seawater failed to prove a discouragement, so warnings were issued about the danger of bad cuts from torn dural by members of the museum staff. It was equally obvious that there would be a rush of souvenir hunters as soon as the aircraft was clear of the water, and divers and museum staff prepared to defend their hard won prize by explaining that it was to go on exhibition, properly restored, at a later date and the public could see it at Brenzett when the work was completed.

By about 2 p.m. the propeller unit had been located near the wreck and a team of divers manhandled the whole unit up the very slippery slope to the sea wall. All three blades had been bent backward by about 20° out of true, and there was speculation about the cause. Was it due to the impact on crashing or to damage sustained during the tow? It was already obvious that a great deal of detective work awaited the museum experts if they were to be able to find out the name of the pilot and the date of the operation. According to official records, there had been over 600 Me 109's shot down in the Channel during the war, few of them had had their sea graves plotted on any charts, and the thirty-six years of sea erosion could well make the finding of vital information almost impossible.

By 2.15 p.m., most of the wing surfaces were uncovered and the engine was found to be lying on the sand beside the leading edge. Its condition was poor, as the cylinder casing had suffered badly from corrosion, but the two banks of valve gear had proved a great attraction for masses of tiny sea shells which could be scraped off with a penknife. There were also two large holes going into the crankcase, which could have been from cannon shells or, possibly, corrosion.

Back on the sea wall, Mrs Buchanan was surprised to see two gentlemen unloading some very expensive audio-vision equipment. Even more amazingly, they admitted to belonging to some obscure department of the Ministry of Defence and had come to make an official record of the beaching. David said that in all the digs the museum had made, this was the first occasion that such interest had been shown. In due course the experts completed their filming and departed silently, roughly in the direction of the "Red Lion" at Hythe. So far, no trace of their film has ever been seen by non-official human eyes.

As the day got hotter, the watching crowd grew. By 3.30 p.m. the JCB digger was able to get to seaward of the aircraft and commenced the digging under the airframe to lift the wings and centre section out of the sand. This operation caused considerable tension to the salvage team, as each gentle push under by the JCB bucket caused a nasty noise of breaking bits and pieces on the aircraft. The driver was reported to have looked like a man who had laid an egg and then inadvertently sat on it, and was now trying to keep the whole affair secret. The army crane started working again and was able to help pull the JCB up toward the sea wall, as the slippery surface was proving too much for its tyres.

As the rest of the wreckage was lifted out of the water, the beachmaster said that he was supposed to be watching the airframe, but found himself concentrating on thousands of tiny crabs and fish which came tumbling out of the wings and fuselage. With museum staff at each wing tip, the aircraft continued up the ramp to the sea wall. Without the engine and tail unit, it looked very small and the full aspect of the corrosion on the undersurface of the wings made the whole thing look like an expensive and time-consuming exercise. Fisherman Alan Griggs got his first view of the aircraft and expressed the opinion that it looked like a corroded pepper pot. Without doubt, he reasoned, he could have made twice as much going fishing instead of embarking on this ridiculous charter operation. Nonetheless, he felt a certain pride in being on both the finding and the recovery of the aircraft, and immediately offered his services for the work of recovering the tail unit from the sea. A businessman to the last, Alan arranged the fee on the spot, reflecting that the livelihood of fishing was full of perils and a man must look to the future. It was as well that he could not visualise that in a further ten months he would find another measure of a fisherman's luck, and that a Government Ministry would propose new safety measures on the country's inshore fishing industry that could cost each fisherman so much that the Minister would be making his intentions known that the Ministry would arrange for the fishermen to pay for the safety measures by instalments.

With the aircraft suspended on the sea wall, the rush of souvenir hunters started, and the two teams had their work cut out to prevent the aircraft being dismantled before their eyes. The police were doing a fine job in crowd control, and Richard Hukins, who had been making a super 8 mm movie of the beaching (from the shore this time) estimated the crowd at nearly two thousand. This was probably to be the peak period for public interest as all could see the Me 109 without being trodden underfoot, as the wreckage was now suspended at eye-level.

David Buchanan recollected that he was worried about the general condition of the airframe. He said, "It looked so fragile, we were afraid that it would fall to pieces when it was swung onto the transporter. The breaking off of the tail unit the previous weekend had almost certainly been due to our underestimating the weight of mud in the aircraft. Our hopes of lifting the Me 109 in one go had been frustrated, but we were most encouraged by the divers' determination to get the missing section ashore at the earliest moment possible."

Getting off the Redoubt for team members became almost as difficult as getting in. David's son, trying to get his car off the site, found the exit gate blocked by a car. When he requested police assistance to move it, the overworked constable told him to find the owner himself. Young Buchanan, with due tact, said he knew who the owner was, as it was a police car blocking the gate. The constable considered this item of news, the hot sweat on his face and the seething mass of people clamouring to get closer to the aircraft. He pronounced his verdict with some force: "If the museum and the divers hadn't insisted on digging up this aircraft, we both wouldn't have a problem. It looks as though you're in for a very long wait."

To assist the police in crowd control, some of the museum staff formed a line and moved back whenever the police asked the crowd to move. In a matter of seconds they found themselves at the back of the crowd. Next they tried forming a human chain and pushed the crowd back. Enjoying the contest, the crowd pushed hard in the opposite direction, so that didn't work. The main police worry was that one of the supporting ropes to the crane would break and that some of the public would get squashed underneath the falling aircraft. To break the deadlock, the police announced that all operations would be suspended unless the crowd did as it was told. The more enterprising members immediately broke away and went onto the beach, reasoning that they were out of police jurisdiction below the tide mark. This doubtful logic did at least break up the main crowd body and split the pressure in another direction.

Some very serious interest was being taken in the aircraft. Museum members were constantly being asked for details of the history, for particulars of the type and, inevitably by some, "Where's the body?" The guns on the aircraft were still 'in situ' and loaded, and although there was little chance of danger from salt saturated ammunition in the conventional terms, those bullets treated as incendiary could possibly become reactivated on contact with the air. These unwanted items of equipment were disposed of by museum officials as soon as possible.

Not unnaturally, Len Green had been first on the spot to try and salvage equipment from the cockpit. His particular interest was in the flight instruments, which, if still readable, might have provided valuable information about the operational state of the aircraft when it ditched. From the underwater reports of the airframe condition, museum staff had been inclined toward the theory that it had been ditched, not crashed. Len found that the instrument panel was now almost non-existent from corrosion and the instruments that had survived the tow ashore were hanging out of the inverted cockpit by wires and mixed in with a miscellaneous cocktail of rubber threads from the decayed safety harness, assorted marine life and wire from the trim unit. After much diligent work, he managed to salvage nine instruments, all badly blackened by water contact. He reflected that the cleaning and restoring of these items could probably take up to a year of someone's spare time. Whether they would reveal any vital information was another matter.

Other members of the museum were checking the flight controls. The control column was almost in two pieces, having rotted badly at the base. The rudder bar was in position and moved freely, the control runs being severed when the tail unit broke away. The engine throttle was set in the idle position, which was also supporting evidence of the engine being throttled back for the ditching. Nobody thought to look at the U/C selector lever, probably assuming that it would be in the U/C open setting. Such a setting would not have supported the theory that the aircraft had been ditched, as the aircraft would certainly have turned on its back on touching down making it very difficult for the pilot to escape. Museum members decided that it would be best to get the aircraft back to New House Farm for cleaning and then make a full examination of all the settings of the flight systems. The entire area of glass surrounding the pilot had vanished, including the front, specially strengthened bullet proof section. There was no radio in the wreckage and this was assumed to be in the unrecovered portion of the aircraft fuselage and tail unit, together with the armoured section, usually positioned behind the fuel tank aft of the pilot.

Later on in the afternoon, the museum staff were strengthened by the arrival of three of their members who had volunteered to keep the museum open to the public that day. One of them, John Elgar Whinney, the group's "map king", was disappointed to learn that no maps or charts had been found.

There was a hitch in the transport arrangements and the expected transporter had not arrived. This tied down the army crane until after 8 p.m. and meanwhile the divers were busy clearing up their equipment and getting the lifting gear, the Me engine and propeller unit stowed on the small lorry for removal to New House Farm.

Gradually the crowd began to drift away and by 8 p.m. the wings had been loaded lengthwise on the contractor's lorry and taken to an overnight stop at his yard. By this time, the divers and museum staff had gradually departed homeward, and David Buchanan found that the beaching site was almost totally deserted, apart from Mrs Buchanan and Len Green. In theory, there should have been some sort of celebration to mark the success of the beaching. In practice, they had all become too tired for the thought to cross anyone's mind.

8 THE AERONAUTICAL ARCHAEOLOGISTS

"The walrus and the carpenter were walking hand in hand. They wept to see such quantities and quantities of sand."

(*Lewis Carroll*)

It is a curious fact that the normal domestic male, when confronted with a request to help with the spring-cleaning at home, will contrive to become invisible to his wife within a matter of seconds. The medical term for this condition is "Domesticus Hiaticus" and there is no known cure. Tell an aeronautical archaeologist that some battered and corroded bits of aircraft, covered inside and out with thirty-six years of mud, sand and marine life require his attention, then another type of human change takes place. His pulse rate will increase, his eye will brighten and his conversation becomes inspired. He will also disappear in the direction of the action at a very high rate of knots. Again, there is no known medical cure, although unexpected call-up for the RAF in a non-flying occupation has been known to effect a temporary relief.

By their own admission, aeronautical archaeologists expect other members of the human race to describe them, at worst, as totally mad, or even eccentric. In fact, they are a lovable bunch of characters who are totally dedicated to the pursuit of aviation history and the extraction of the last grain of truth from a crumbling wreck. These men are drawn from all walks of life and are often gifted with the power to restore battered metal objects to their original pristine condition. Others of their number have been known to write long technical reports on subjects which bear no relation to their professional calling, or to be found in swamp-saturated ground up to the waist in mud and soaked from pouring rain, digging manfully for two hundredweight of aero engine. They will admit, if asked, to being both cold and miserable, but will conceive no reason as to why they should be elsewhere at that moment in time.

In the week following the beaching of the Me 109, group members could be found working away at the mammoth task of steam cleaning the inside and outside of the wreckage. The penetration of the mud in one wing was so compacted that it took ten members to lift it down from the transporter. Normally four could have managed it quite easily. It was the intention of the group to strip down the airframe to its basic components, and clean each part individually to get rid of all the salt and dirt. When any metal structure is brought out of the sea after a long period of immersion, the rate of corrosion increases enormously and unless suitably treated will be reduced to a useless pile of scrap within months. The treatment is drastic. After cleaning, the metal has to be cleared from all existing corrosion. The next process involves treatment with a de-watering fluid, or by a preventative oil mist. However, after a few months some of the remaining salt usually found in concentration at the base of the rivet heads will begin to reactivate and will commence the popping out of the rivets at unexpected moments. Additional treatment is then urgently required to contain the preservation.

By the end of August, the airframe had been cleaned, stripped, labelled and stored, awaiting full restoration. Ideally, a very dry shed with little water content in the air would have been desirable. Unfortunately, the barn in which the aircraft had to be stored was not dry, and in six months the sound of popping rivets could be heard at dead of night, giving the place the quite undeserved reputation of being haunted.

During the period of the stripping and labelling of parts, David Buchanan and his team began the massive problem of tracing the origin of the aircraft. To the dedicated aircraft historian, there are two clear paths available to him and it is usual to try and use both, cross-checking one source against the other.

The first and easiest method of checking is to locate part numbers relating to the aircraft against existing German records. There are a few British books which publish details of the German records, F. K. Mason's work, "Battle over Britain", being considered the bible of the aeronautical archaeologist. This method is usually considered to be reliable, but like all systems must be open to suspicion. First, the records could be wrong or out of date. That is not an indictment of Mason, who would probably be the first to admit his fallibility. During the period of June to November in 1940, the German airforce was constantly on the move across Europe and new operational bases were being established almost daily. Operational squadrons suffered losses both in aircraft and pilots at a very high rate. Other aircraft returned to base in a damaged condition and airframes and engines had to be replaced with new parts when possible. Sometimes undamaged parts from crashes were used to repair other aircraft when spares were in short supply, and although the German storekeeping was very methodical, they were quite capable of making errors – especially when under pressure from enemy action. The whole system was dedicated first to keeping the aircraft operational so that the maximum number of aircraft could be used every day; secondly, it was not unknown for a pilot to have a last minute serviceability failure before an operation and take the spare aircraft for one trip. If he failed to return, then someone else could take his aircraft for the next sortie. If the first pilot returned to his squadron, say after ditching in the Channel, then he might demand his old aircraft back. The storekeeper's records would record the change, but could well suffer from a time lag in making the entries. Engines were often changed during battle conditions to allow the hard-pressed mechanics time to effect lengthy repairs. Records of engine numbers and airframe numbers do not guarantee a pair for the operational life of the 'plane.

David's first checks had given him an engine number to work from, and the records suggested that its last flight could have been after July, 1940. This was rightly considered inconclusive, and a renewed search was made for the more reliable airframe number. The search revealed a large variety of individual part numbers including that of the undercarriage, but the airframe number eluded them. Beachmaster Peter Foote came to the rescue by providing the location of the airframe number on his own Me 109, which was underneath two long side strips that formed part of the wing attachment area. He also thought that the rather high undercarriage number they had found suggested that the aircraft had been made by a sub-contractor.

The team began the search again and an Arado manufacturer's plate was found on one of the wing spars. The number on this plate provided cross-links with the German records and seemed to point to the German pilot being a certain Erich Meyer.

This was to be the first real lead that the group were able to use in the writing of the museum history of the Me 109. During 1975 the museum had been optimistic that the aircraft might prove to be the one shot down in September, 1940, which was seen to belly-land in the sea off Hythe. This aircraft had been chased over the coast at sea level by a Spitfire. Unfortunately, there was no evidence to support this story and, when the Me 109 was salvaged in 1976, all the evidence began to point in another direction.

David's German contact, Herr Kirchner, sent over details of Me 109 losses for August to October, 1940, which were known to have crash landed in the sea off the area of Folkestone/Lydd; and by a gentle process of elimination, David was able to narrow the possible candidates down to two. The dates were August, 4, 1940 and October 7. The pilots named were Lt. Reinegan and Lt. Meyer respectively. Both had flown Me 109's and both had come down in the sea within five miles of the area where the wreck had been found. The link-up of the airframe number of 4853 with Lt. Meyer was positive evidence and made further checks on Meyer's operational history the first priority.

As the German records suggested that Lt. Meyer had been taken to a POW camp in England, having survived the ditching after his last operation, David realised that there was a fifty-fifty chance that he might still be alive. The next problem was to find him. After thirty-six years he might be living anywhere in the world. Obviously the best place to start the search was in Germany, and Kirchner was asked to undertake the task.

The next place to start looking was in England. Perhaps witnesses of the events of October 7, 1940 might be found still living on the coast. Possibly Meyer had been picked up by lifeboat or air/sea rescue, and some of the official records might still survive. Group members could be found asking questions of local inhabitants during the next few weeks, but nothing of interest was discovered. A search of the Dungeness lifeboat records for the period did seem to provide another lead and the following extract gave the researchers considerable food for thought:—

7 October, 1940
"At 2.10 p.m. information was received by telephone that a fighter aircraft had crashed in the sea. A few minutes later, one of the lifeboat men reported that he could see a small object on the water. A light westerly breeze was blowing with a moderate sea. The motor lifeboat 'Charles Cooper Henderson' was launched at 2.25 p.m. and 3 miles to the NE by E of the lifeboat station found a German pilot in a small rubber boat. He was taken into the lifeboat, disarmed, his head injuries dressed, and landed at the station at 3.25 p.m., where a military escort awaited him. Rewards: £15 15s."

The cox was believed to be C. W. D. Oyler, but the RNLI were not able to confirm this.

The report was historically interesting, but did not contain the name of the rescued pilot. What it did tell the museum was that the pilot had been injured and armed when found, and that he had taken to his dinghy. It also gave the position of the dinghy to be a good deal further to the west than the site of the wreckage had led them to expect. Perhaps the most vital piece of information contained in the report was the time of the crash and the weather report – "a light westerly breeze and a moderate sea". Was this the missing Lt. Meyer?

At first, David was inclined to think that this was indeed the case.

By December, 1976, the group had learnt a great deal about the wreckage. The story revealed by the cleaning of the parts had enabled the group to commence the other part of the investigation, which was to consider the "probable cause" of the crash landing. There were five possibilities: first, fighter interception from the RAF had terminated the operation; secondly, ground fire from coastal batteries; thirdly, the question of a mechanical defect had to be considered; fourth, in the absence of the pilot, the question had to be asked, "Had he baled out?" Finally, had the aircraft come down simply because the fuel tanks were empty?

The last cause was the most likely if the aircraft was used in its operational role as a fighter bomber. Carrying the normal bomb load of one 250 kg bomb to London and with full tanks, the Me 109 E, if operating from Northern France, would only have about ten minutes' flying time in the target area. If the aircraft was intercepted by the RAF, then the pilot would be using maximum power to 'dog-fight' and his reserve would vanish at a much faster rate.

Examination of the engine showed that, although badly corroded, it had not been hit by gunfire. The pistons were all seized, however, so the engine had certainly failed. Bullet strikes found in the wing radiators would have allowed all the engine coolant to escape. The angle of penetration of the bullets suggested that they had come from slightly below and behind the Me. The bullets were British 303 calibre and could have been fired from an aircraft or from a very lucky Light AA gunner on the ground. On average, another fighter aircraft seemed the right answer, unless the Me had been flying below 200 ft at the time of the strikes.

Again, it seemed unlikely that the pilot had baled out. Examination of the cockpit failed to reveal any sign of the pilot. Also conspicuous by their absence were the parachute, life-jacket and the rubber dinghy. There was no sign of the flare pistol, but some rotted cartridges were found in the rack.

Unfortunately the pilot's safety harness had also rotted away. The harness attachment points, however, being metal, were in good condition, showing no evidence of heavy G forces being applied. If the pilot had baled out, then this would be expected. If the pilot had ditched in the aircraft, then the anchorage was designed for just this type of impact and might be undamaged or slightly deformed. If the aircraft had crashed into the sea, out of control, then the G forces would have been so high that the straps would certainly have broken and the attachment points damaged. Inevitably, the pilot would have been projected forward, and if his feet were still on the rudder bar some evidence of bending or fracture of the control would have been found here. A high speed, out of control impact with the sea would have almost certainly caused the aircraft structure to break, tearing off the wings in a backward and upward direction and breaking off the tail. The aircraft structure had been intact when examined by the divers.

The probability was that the aircraft had been ditched by the pilot and that he had used his dinghy to escape.

There was one glaring snag to the theory that the aircraft had been ditched. The examination of the control settings had shown that the wing slots were out and locked, the engine had been throttled back, the flaps were able to move freely when examined and could have been at almost any setting. So far so good. It was that Churchillian gesture of the undercarriage in the down and locked position that seemed to confound the theory of a ditching. If the Me had ditched with its undercarriage down, it would have certainly acted as a violent brake to forward motion, just forward of the centre of gravity and several feet *below* the main forward motion of the aircraft. The aircraft would have instantly flipped over onto its back, the rear tail plane would have been ripped off, the fracture being in the direction of the supporting struts.

The wreckage did not confirm that this had happened. No pilot would deliberately ditch his aircraft with the undercarriage down. The aircraft condition suggested that the undercarriage had opened underwater when the aircraft was lying on its back, but there was no evidence to show how this could have happened.

9 THE GENTLE ART OF DEDUCTION

"When I looked at my old man's shirt next morning, the lipstick smears made it obvious that he had been playing tarts – not darts!"

(*Housewife*)

The examination of the wreckage of any aircraft is a complex task. The museum group and the divers had recovered a thirty-six year old aircraft that had looked relatively intact when dug out of the sand on the sea bed. By the time the aircraft had been brought into store at New House Farm, it had suffered considerable damage. It had lost about a third of the rear fuselage including the tail control surfaces; the cockpit canopy had vanished; the engine had come free from its bearers and the propeller unit had separated from the engine.

To analyse the wreckage correctly, it would be necessary to decide on the time scale of wreckage disintegration.

All the evidence from the report on Lt. Meyer (the first verbal report from Germany) pointed to the aircraft having to ditch in the Channel because the engine seized after total coolant loss sustained during air combat.

Assuming the pilot had been able to follow normal ditching procedures, the aircraft had ditched with its undercarriage up. The pilot had then used his dinghy to escape and been picked up by either a lifeboat (Dungeness) or by an air/sea rescue unit. The aircraft, left to its own devices, had then sunk. The nose, being the heaviest part, would have sunk first, and, if the 109 had landed in the position where it was found by the divers, then it must have nosed over the vertical on the way down and finished up on its back.

So when did the undercarriage open? Did the pilot deliberately lower the U/C after he ditched, allowing water to enter the U/C housing in the wing to ensure that the aircraft would sink? Or did it open when the aircraft was resting upside down on the sea bed and, if so, what caused it to open? The problem was complicated by the natural assumption that the pilot would switch off all electric systems before he ditched. No trace of the undercarriage fairings had been found by the divers, so again it had to be assumed that they had been torn off by the force of the impact. To David, making his mental reconstruction of the past events, there seemed to be a great deal too many assumptions being made.

Again, if the actual date of the ditching had been October 7, 1940, what damage had been sustained by the airframe underwater until rediscovered by fisherman Alan Griggs in 1974? Storms could have damaged the airframe for a start, unless the sea bed suction had dragged it down during the first few days of immersion. If that was the case, then the wide area of the wings would probably have stopped further sinking of the airframe and the light silt covering of the top of the wings made sense.

Remembering the divers' reports of the wreckage area, David recalled that they had reported seeing trawl chains entangled in the wreck. Alan Griggs had said clearly that the underwater obstruction was well known to local fishermen, who had caught their nets on it in the past. Could these chains have dragged the U/C out of its housings? He made a mental note to take another look at the undercarriage to see if there were any major damage marks near the wheel hubs. It seemed a bit unlikely that this had happened. After all, the undercarriage had a mechanical lock in both the up and down positions, and this would be difficult to break unless two separate trawls had been made in opposite directions along the actual wing surfaces. If that had happened, he would certainly find evidence of the over-riding of the mechanical U/C lock in the wreckage. Could the marine life below water have entered the cockpit and altered the setting of the undercarriage selection lever? This sounded wildly unlikely to David. Could a pressure bottle (oxygen bottle) have exploded and altered the lever setting? That sounded even worse.

Anyway, would there have been any power to actuate the U/C? David thought not.*

David was faced with a problem by the unexpected behaviour of the Me 109 undercarriage. Either the U/C was closed when the aircraft ditched, unless the pilot was attempting to land on a sandbank, or, if it had been open, then the wreck should be able to produce evidence of this, by virtue of damage which would be sustained by the airframe on the inevitable flick onto its back when it hit the water. Clearly further work would have to be done by the group before this section of the mystery was resolved.

Continuing his time scale of past events, David reasoned that once the aircraft became cocooned in the clay bed beneath the sand, structural damage was almost stopped and the onset of corrosion delayed. Not only was the airframe sealed in the clay externally, but every small hollow area had been given a natural injection of clay, sand and marine life. Unfortunately there was no immediate evidence to show how many of the thirty-six years underwater had been spent in the cocooned state.

The trawl chains found on the aircraft might provide a further clue if the owners could be traced. They would certainly remember when they lost their nets in the opened

---

* This mental speculation is as necessary to the accredited Accident Investigation Inspector as it is to the searcher after truths in other walks of life. In criminal investigation the committer of a crime does not usually send a written statement to the detective in charge, advising him in detail of all his individual actions leading up to the crime. The accredited Investigation Officer of aircraft accidents in this country is usually employed by a department of the Department of Industry. He may have been previously employed for many years as an airline pilot, or have been a serving officer in the RAF. Other members of the team have served their time in the engineering or electrical branches of aviation. Some may have been recruited from air traffic control work. There are many areas today where special experience is used in the investigation of flying accidents. The resources of learned scientific bodies are always at the disposal of the professional investigator. Even then, members of this team have not always found out the full truth about certain of their investigations. When their reports are submitted at an inquiry, they nearly always contain the words, "The probable cause . . ."

undercarriage, and it would be safe to assume that the U/C had been opened *before* that date. Here was another lead to follow up; perhaps the divers would already know when those other nets had been lost.

David let his mind move forward over the time scale again. So far as he knew, apart from the trawl chains, nothing had touched the wreck underwater until Alan Griggs had caught his nets on the U/C in 1974. The next event was the actual discovery by the divers, and all they had been able to see was the undercarriage and airscrew blade above the sand. When Len Green had gone out with them the next weekend, they had found some odd bits lying about on the sand near the wreck. There was the connector plug, and part of the pitot head from the wing, and what they thought had been a small generator. That was all. It was the middle of the first diving season that they had identified the type of aircraft for certain, when the divers had uncovered the DB engine and classified it from the exhaust stubs. David remembered Jess saying that the 'plane appeared to have sunk into the clay very early on after the crash. The clay covering the wreck did not look as if it had been accumulated by the tides.

By 1975 mid season, the divers had excavated almost down to the rim of the cockpit. That would have been about six feet down in the clay. Apart from the starboard radiator, he could not remember anyone bringing up any parts of the aircraft during that season. He was sure that Jess had said that the aircraft was complete, and both Jess and Big Graham had said that the skin of the fuselage had been intact where they touched it. Little Graham had mentioned that one place on the skin about two feet behind the wings had seemed weaker than the rest and the panels could be made to move by hand, but not to separate. Some rivets had been missing, he said, but he had been positive that there was no major crack in the skin. David thought that Jess had mentioned another item about this time. Something to do with the tail plane struts. One of them wasn't located correctly in its socket by the tail wheel and the tail wheel was never found. That was what he said at the time, but, looking back, David began to wonder when the tail wheel was lost from the fuselage. Had it been during the ditching? Or was the tail wheel retractable on the 109 E4 and not noticed by the divers? Something else to check on, as

Bf 109-4/B of II/JG 54 in post-Battle of Britain finish and markings. (*Courtesy of Macdonald & Jane's Publishers Ltd.*)

Divers over wreck site, 1½ miles out to sea. (*Courtesy of Brenzett Aeronautical Museum*)

Divers' team leader Jess Henderson goes over the side. (*Courtesy of Brenzett Aeronautical Museum*)

The first item to come from the seabed and identified by Len Green as German. Plug and socket are shown separated. (*Courtesy of G. Cardew*)

Aircraft Werk No. on Messerschmitt Bf 109E–4/B. Sub-contractor, Arado.

The coastguard called out this helicopter to search for the missing diver (see page 55). (*Courtesy of R. Freeman, Brenzett Aeronautical Museum*)

The "Opportunity" with divers inflatables to port and starboard. (*Courtesy of Brenzett Aeronautical Museum*)

Aircraft still submerged but with crane wire attached. (*Courtesy of Brenzett Aeronautical Museum*)

First parts of the aircraft to see the light of day after 37 years on the seabed. (*Courtesy of Brenzett Aeronautical Museum*)

Spectators begin to crowd in on the workers. (*Courtesy of Brenzett Aeronautical Museum*)

Picture shows engine beside leading edge of wing. (*Courtesy of B. Abbott*)

Removing the engine from the aircraft. (*Courtesy of Brenzett Aeronautical Museum*)

Divers manhandling the propeller unit ashore. (*Courtesy of Brenzett Aeronautical Museum*)

Wreckage of wings and centre section still inverted, being brought up the ramp by JCB and crane. (*Courtesy of Brenzett Aeronautical Museum*)

Wings and fuselage being manhandled into position. Cross is just visible on underside of starboard wing. (*Courtesy of J. Pope*)

The aircraft before lifting onto the sea wall. Note instruments on ends of cables trailing below the cockpit. The engine and prop. unit are already ashore – but guns are still "in situ".
(*Courtesy of P. Mallett*)

Cleaning up the wing at Newhouse Farm. *Left to right:* David Buchanan with R. Hukins and R. Freeman. (*Courtesy of Kentish Express*)

Radiator core. Photo shows two dark spots where bullets entered.

Propeller unit complete. Blade on left of photo shows bullet hole.

Port wing inverted. Photo clearly shows good condition of attachment bolt sockets. Leading edge is to left of picture.

Front view of engine with reduction gears and prop. unit removed.

Centre section standing right way up for once.

Looking at the rear of the centre section. This area contained the fuel tank which had rotted away. The long shaft and disc is the fuel pump. Note bright metal on right hand side where tail unit broke away.

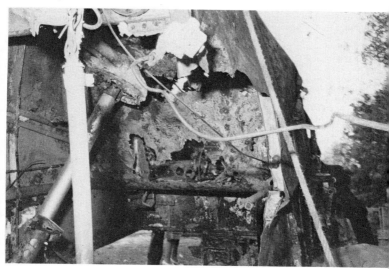

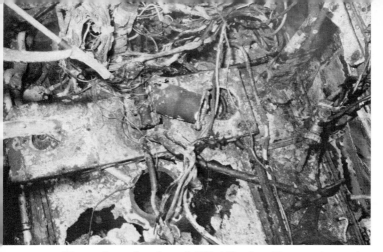

Photo shows interior of ME 109 after 37 years immersion.

David Buchanan shows off DB engine after first cleaning. Marine life and holes in casing are still in evidence.

The two diving Hendersons (unrelated); Jess having grown a beard by 1977.

The two team leaders. *Left:* Jess Henderson (divers) and *right:* David Buchanan (Museum).

Some of the Brenzett Aeronautical Museum team trying to sort out a six-page accident investigation questionnaire.

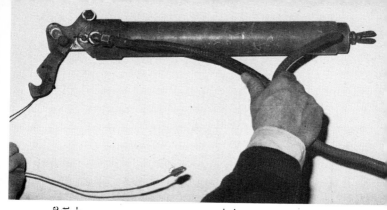

Right: Shows the up-locks on the under-carriage mechanism.

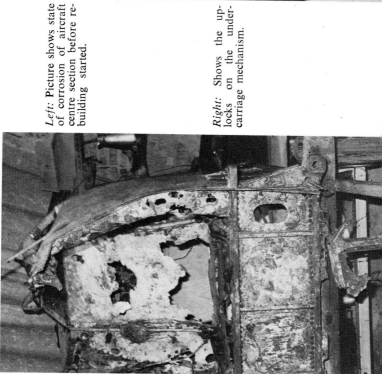

Left: Picture shows state of corrosion of aircraft centre section before re-building started.

Starting rebuilding. Wing centre section front cockpit floor. (*Courtesy of D. Buchanan, Brenzett Aeronautical Museum*)

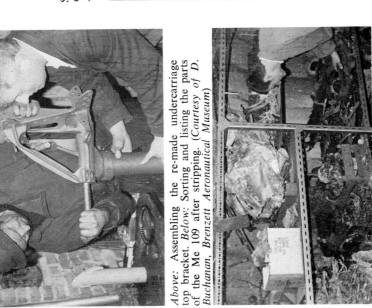

Above: Assembling the re-made undercarriage top bracket. *Below*: Sorting and listing the parts of the Me 109 after stripping. (*Courtesy of D. Buchanan, Brenzett Aeronautical Museum*)

The pilot of The Reluctant Messerschmitt, Lt. Meyer, being congratulated at the end of a successful sortie.

MacKenzie, Holden, Daffern and Ginger Lacey who posed rather self consciously for a visiting artist at RAF Station Filton in January 1941. (*Courtesy of W/C MacKenzie Collection*)

This Squadron photo of 501 was taken at Kenley in October 1940. Not all the pilots were named, but P/O MacKenzie and Sgt Ginger Lacey are in the right hand front row. Centre of middle row: the C/O S/Ldr Hogan with Fl/Lt Holden on his right. (*Courtesy of W/C MacKenzie Collection*)

the symptoms were not unlike those of an aircraft that had flipped over on its back after ditching. There again, the tail wheel could have been pulled off by a trawl chain, causing similar damage.

The temptation at that moment to say, "If the pilot flying aircraft No. 4853, engine No. 64688 Me 109 E4. Sub-contractor Arado, was Lt. Meyer, and we have found an airframe of a Me 109 E4 using these numbers, then this airframe must have been the one used on the operation on October 7, 1940," was nearly irresistible to David. The positive proof would have to rest with the full report from the German pilot. Would his ditching sequence tie up with the evidence found underwater by the divers?

Reluctantly, David brought his thoughts back to the time sequence. The first time that the aircraft had been moved by the divers had been on July 18, 1976, when the trawler had towed the Me for about 50 yards. There hadn't been enough lift and the movement had been more in the nature of an irregular scrape along the sea bed. On July 19, the wreck had actually lifted to within 18 feet of the surface and was towed to within $\frac{1}{2}$ mile of the shore, losing the tail and breaking the engine bearers in the process. The engine and propeller unit had remained joined up to that time. Somewhere during these two days, some of the aircraft instruments had probably fallen out of the floating but inverted cockpit. David wondered if the divers would be able to find the same place again underwater without the major portion of the aircraft to guide them.

The next move on the time scale was on Sunday, July 25, when the final lift took place. Here the prop unit parted company with the engine, and when the wreck was being brought up the ramp by the JCB, some damage had resulted due to the action of lifting the airframe. Paintwork, or what was left of it, was going to provide a number of scars, both old and new, which would help in deciding the time scale of damage. The group members had looked carefully to see if there were any signs of an 'in-flight fire'. This sort of occurrence usually leaves a rearward trail of small molten particles firmly attached to the fuselage. Engine failure by loss of cooling liquid could produce just such a fire. Lt. Meyer had been rather lucky, it would seem, as no such traces were found.

Movement of the airframe to New House Farm would have also provided a trail of new marks on the wreckage, and there was no way of remembering how many times the jets of the steam cleaners they had used had punched holes in the corroded skin. Any damage after the cleaning would have been the direct result of stripping down the airframe and tagging each bit for future reference. To develop a simple rule of thumb, David decided to concentrate on old damage marks. Marks that were recent would be bright and those that were old would have been subject to obvious sea action. That, at least, would be a fair guide to damage that occurred during the ditching.

Members of the group had already taken home bits of wreckage to get on with the work of restoration. Three of the old exhaust stubs already looked new after being descaled, chemically cleaned and given a brand new coat of metallic paint. Work was proceeding apace on the broken base of the control column, and the instrument experts had already cleaned and reassembled such instruments as had been recovered. Sadly, the latter had offered no chance of obtaining readings from the crash settings.

The group had decided to make the total restoration of the airframe a long-term objective, more in the nature of a five-year spare time plan. Initially, it was decided that they would restore the cockpit and engine area to have something to show visitors to the museum. David would have to complete his examination very quickly, or there would be little evidence left to provide clues.

On his next visit to New House Farm, David made a thorough examination of the wreckage again. This must be about the thirtieth time, thought David, as he critically examined the bent propeller blades. They still looked the same, bent back 20° gradually from the thickest part of the blades to a tip angle of about 70° out of true. The pitch setting had to be considered unreliable, as the blades could be moved by hand. The tips of the blades showed evidence of fragmentation and the small holes, one each in two of the blades, could have been bullets from the same burst of gunfire that hit the wing radiator. The entry point was at the rear of the blade.

That burst of gunfire did a lot of damage, reflected David.

After all, the attacker came from below and behind and most of the burst must have gone below the aircraft. This had to be the case because there were no strikes on the fuselage. David paused, unsure of the logic of this statement. Perhaps it was a very short burst? The Me pilot would have certainly taken violent evasive action at the first hits, assuming he hadn't spotted his attacker. If he had spotted him, then he must have pushed the stick forward, diving away over the vertical. That was the usual drill, because the Me 109 could outdive a Spitfire or Hurricane as the fuel systems they used didn't like the sudden negative G.

So far, there was only evidence of four actual bullet strikes, two in the radiator and two in the propeller. But suppose there had been strikes in the tail and rear fuselage, these might have been stopped by the armour plate guarding the fuel tank and the pilot from the rear. That evidence was still on the sea bed. If the radio receiver was still in the tail, perhaps the strikes could have caused loss of contact with the rest of the squadron at the time. If only there was some way to establish at what height the bullet strikes occurred. Operational heights were often around 20,000 feet at that period of the Battle of Britain, so if the action was at this height, then the pilot would have about twenty miles to glide with a dead engine. Alternatively, if the combat was near the coast, he might have just made it back to France. If the combat was inland, such a course of action was beyond the range of the aircraft, and a Channel ditching was the probable result.

The finding of the wreck about $1\frac{1}{2}$ miles from the shore gave credence to the possibility of an inland dog-fight, perhaps in the bombing area. The London docks had been a favourite target about this time. From the look of the wreckage under the cockpit area, there was no scrap of evidence of a fire. From the non-separation of the wreckage when found underwater, the pilot must have had the use of his flying controls when ditching. The numbers on the airframe had certainly belonged to Lt. Meyer. David again considered the position of the crashed aircraft. If the wreckage had sunk into the mud immediately after ditching, it was five miles to the east of the lifeboat pick-up. True, the report also said that the winds were light and westerly. So how long would it take a life raft to drift five miles? Perhaps one or two hours. He checked back to the lifeboat report. The crash into the sea happened close to two o'clock and the lifeboat was back at its station in less than one and a half hours. It must follow that the lifeboat couldn't have picked up Meyer in the time available, and must have picked up another pilot. This reasoning shook David's confidence for a moment. Who was the other pilot? Was he involved in the same operation as Meyer? Worse still, why were there no lifeboat records recording Meyer's pick-up, because he was certainly made a prisoner-of-war on October 7, 1940?

The obvious answer to the last question was that the RAF or the Navy had made a pick-up. That meant more historic records for David to check. It also meant that the museum might reasonably expect to find another German fighter 'plane, just east of the area of the lifeboat pick-up, five miles nearer to Dungeness.

10 THE FINAL DECISIONS

By April, 1977, a report had been received from Germany which originated from Lt. Meyer. The translation from German to English lost a lot, as is inevitable in semi-technical work, but the final report clearly tied up with most of the findings made by the museum staff. Some of the findings by the museum were very clear-cut and left them in no doubt at all that Lt. Meyer was, indeed, the pilot of the Me 109 E4 now in their possession. The report did not, however, give details of the actual time of the raid over London and the subsequent air battle, nor could it identify the pilot who shot him down, although the date of the action was correct. Meyer certainly ditched (undercarriage up) within 400 yards from the spot his aircraft was found and said that it was about two hours and 20 minutes before he was picked up by two patrol boats, after being spotted by a Lysander aircraft. They took him to Dover, thereby shattering the hopes that the report by

104

the Dungeness lifeboat crew applied to Meyer. Clearly it applied to another Me 109, and Meyer recalled that one of his comrades had ditched about a mile to his west after he had been in the water about five minutes.*

Meyer's report left David Buchanan and his group with a considerable amount of research still to be made. First, the actual time of the raid had to be established. Then the British pilots identified and, if still alive, to be found and asked about their part in the action. Somewhere there had to be a report by an air/sea rescue launch that had picked up the German pilot, and a sighting report from the pilot of the Lysander aircraft. The missing items of survival equipment had to be accounted for, and the divers still had the problem of trying to relocate the tail unit of the aircraft to check for bullet damage and frequency setting of the radio. Finally, there was the curious behaviour of the undercarriage opening under water, which seemed to set a most unusual problem as no existing technical literature had recorded anything quite like this phenomena before. To complicate the problems of research, the public records office, which housed many of the 1939/45 war records, was in the throes of moving from Chancery Lane to Kew and many vital documents were unavailable for scrutiny for a period of many months.

The task of tracing the British pilots was simplified by the use of Mason's book, "Battle over Britain", which listed methodically all the German aircraft shot down day-by-day during the battle and also recorded, where known, the names of the British pilots officially credited with their demise. David's interest focussed on the activities of 501 Squadron, based at Kenley, on October 7, 1940.

Air Historian Peter Cornwell had credited S/Ldr. Hogan and a P/O Mackenzie with a shared victory on Meyer's aircraft. Both pilots were from 501 Sqdn. F. K. Mason's book specifically credited Meyer's downfall to a F/Lt. Holden, also of 501 Sqdn, but during the 10.15 interception on the same

* The author found so much detail lacking from the report that, after gathering material from many other sources, he reconstructed the events of Meyer's last flight and rewrote it in the style of 1940, adding many details about the handling of the Me 109 and also other eye-witness reports on the flight. This report is contained in the second part of the book.

day. The C/O of 501 Squadron was S/Ldr. Hogan. The unit was equipped with Hurricanes. Not unnaturally, David had no means of knowing if any of these pilots had survived the war, or indeed would still be alive in 1977. He also had no means of knowing if they would want to talk about their experiences if they were still alive, but the itch to get at the full story of the museum's exhibit could not be resisted. Letters were duly dispatched to the Ministry of Defence and also to the Battle of Britain Fighter Pilots' Association in the rather forlorn hope that somebody would be able to help.

During the waiting that followed, a meeting was arranged for members of the group on May 20, 1977, to try to co-ordinate the findings of members over the last three years and to make sure that no evidence had been missed that might have any bearing on the final history of the exhibit.

Some sixteen aeronautical archaeologists turned up to put their amateur status to the test, together with Jess Henderson from the divers group to keep tabs on the underwater side of things. The long room of New House Farm looked full to overflowing, the old oak beams getting a further smoke curing treatment from an assortment of pipes and cigarettes. Richard Hukins started the ball rolling with a description of the towing operation as seen from the air. One of the instructors from the Lydd flying club, Don Peak, had taken Richard up in the club's Cessna 150 on Saturday, July 17. Richard said that although his cine camera had a small zoom lens, they had to go as low as 60 feet over the water to get any detail. As the tow was proceeding at about 4 mph, this entailed leaning out of the aircraft window banked at about 80° to keep the water-borne procession in the viewfinder. After a few minutes, they found salt spray coming in and had to shut the window and climb a bit before resuming the shooting. On Sunday, 18th, Richard went up with Neil Sharpe, but the water operation had to be abandoned because of firing from the army ranges. On the final day of the beaching, Richard had been filming from the beach. The films had been seen previously by group members, but a repeat showing of the beaching was demanded. Unfortunately this had to be deferred owing to a dud lamp in the projector. To get members thinking about the recovery work, they were then divided into groups of three and each group handed a large and highly technical questionnaire about five pages thick, based on many of the usual questions that have to be answered during an official accident investigation* by Government crash investigators. This produced some worried frowns from members who hadn't had to cope with anything like this before, and demands to take the forms home before final completion could be heard from all sides of the room.

Most members had their own way of keeping records of what had happened over the last three years so this was agreed. When the forms were analysed two weeks later, at least two of the groups had provided very accurate answers to most of the questions, and the overall picture emerging added several bits of useful information which had not been generally known before. One of the final questions on the form had asked members to offer their own theory on why the 109's undercarriage had opened under water, and two groups came out with an interesting theory.

They suggested that the aircraft had laid underwater for a few days with the undercarriage closed and that, during this time, the action of the sea water had released the hydraulic fluid content. The air in the tyres would be exerting an upward force on the undercarriage, still in the wings, and, because of the underwater pressure difference at 40 feet, would lift the wheels out of the housing to the open position where the mechanical U/C down-lock would operate automatically. The wheels, being made of magnesium, would dissolve quickly in the seawater, thus freeing the tyres from the rims, leaving only the axle stubs as found by the divers.

It was an ingenious theory, but ignored the mechanical uplocks fitted to the aircraft. It was agreed that professional advice might be sought on this point. The time factor was unknown for the action of the sea water on magnesium, nor was it understood how sea water could get into the hydraulic reservoir so quickly.

The later part of the evening had been left open for general discussion, and the form-filling exercises provided a number of points for argument. Len Green raised doubts about the official figure of 601 Me's being shot down in the Channel during the Battle of Britain. He thought the total was probably

* See appendix

107

nearer to 500 for the Battle, the higher figure being for th
duration of the war.

Denis Timms recalled that the actual work of clearing th
beaching point from large rocks had posed a number of publi
relations problems with the public. When members were seer
carrying large rocks over to the next set of breakwaters and
then dumping them, people would stroll across and ask, "Why
are you moving that rock?" At first members tried to explain
that they were going to beach a wartime Messerschmitt at the
Redoubt, and wanted a clear run for the tow-in. According to
Denis, the usual reaction to this information was one of tota
disbelief. The seekers after information would then usually
walk away rapidly, taking quick glances over their shoulders
in case they were being followed. Denis said that they all go
tired of this implied lack of personal credibility and resorted
to subterfuge, saying that they were all keep-fit enthusiast
and were doing it for exercise. This reply was always considered acceptable.

Malcolm Timms (son of Denis) volunteered the unexpected
information that he and his father had both joined the ranks
of the Aeronautical Society, following the visit of a Mr
Boswell, then leader of the Ashford Group, who had called to
borrow the family van to move some large chunks of excavated aircraft. The Timms family were much intrigued by the
specimens and offered their help to the society, despite Mr
Boswell's anti-recruiting propaganda. This consisted largely of
such phrases as "You've got to know your stuff on aircraft or
you'll never stick it." The Timm's family were already equipped
with a library of aeronautical books, all well thumbed, and
managed to convince the sceptical Mr Boswell of their
potential value as members of his society.

Denis Timms gave his version of a dig that happened about
a year later which bore out some of the illustrious Mr Boswell's reservations. The crash was a second world war aircraft
and was located on an isolated part of a private estate belonging to an Army Major. Unfortunately, he would not allow a
mechanical digger to be used by the group and the recovery
area was in woodland set all around with swamp, and none of
the trees had been cut down or cleared for many years. When
they set to work, members were subjected to prolonged spells
of dive bombing by mosquitoes, which Denis swore were all

about three inches long. The group tried mosquito repellent, but the insects seemed to feed on it, so they changed to antihystamine creams, but they didn't work either. Everyone came out in lumps or sores, with Denis claiming a personal record of thirty-six bites. He commented, "We dug the aircraft up, but we never got it out. No one would go back and work in there."

Members had some hard views about the way the Me 109 E4 had been recovered from the sea, and several clear lessons had emerged from this first underwater exercise. Group Treasurer, Denis Timms, said that it cost too much* and suggested alternative methods of lifting underwater crashes more economically.

They all agreed that they had grossly underestimated the actual weight of the aircraft after thirty-seven years underwater, and said that this was the major factor in the break-off of the tail unit. Having got 70 per cent of the wreck ashore, the next major problem was its preservation and restoration, which was probably going to take five years before completion. The primary objective of the group had to be a suitable museum exhibit, and it was suggested that the cockpit, engine and undercarriage might well be restored in time for the 1978 season.

All members were full of praise for the work of the diving team over a long and difficult period of underwater operations. Team leader Jess promised that work on the recovery of the tail unit would start as soon as possible in 1977, but warned that this small part of the wreck might well change its position during the winter storms.

In so far as the final part of the story of the Me's last flight was concerned, it was felt that the museum would be lucky if they actually discovered the whereabouts of any of the surviving British pilots involved in the operation of October 7, 1940. It was really stretching their luck to hope for the discovery of the pilot who actually shot down the Messerschmitt when about sixty aircraft must have been milling around in the dogfight after the bombs had been dropped. The time taken to shoot down an aircraft was usually measured in seconds, not minutes, and identification of individual pilots relied on eye-

* See appendix

witness reports from other pilots, all usually heavily committed to keeping their own tails out of trouble.

In the case of the Messerschmitt, the identification of the pilot could only come from the German side in their description of the combat. As David Buchanan put it after the meeting closed, "Members look like having a very full year's work ahead of them."

11 THE REBUILDING OF MEYER'S MESSERSCHMITT

When the aircraft had been recovered from the sea, many observers felt that the task of reconstruction of the remains would be far beyond the resources of the Museum Group. For their part, members felt that the effort was too important not to at least, try their luck.

During the initial cleaning of the wreckage, the first job had been to pressure out all the mud and sand from the wings and fuselage. This work could only be done properly if some of the wing panels were unriveted to allow access to all the cavities and the control rod conduits. After the steam cleaning was completed the aircraft was left for twenty four hours to allow the salt and accumulated muck to sweat out of all the riveted joints. This steaming and drying process had been repeated three times, and the aircraft was then given a total spray treatment with a very light penetrating oil.

The whole of the cockpit area was then very carefully photographed from different directions so that no individual part should remain unrecorded. After this operation had been completed, the next step was to examine the airframe to record details of every part number that could be seen. The actual "works number" of the aircraft was found to be in two places on the wreckage available, one being located from under the wing fairing at the fuselage joint and the other from the busbar from the electrical switchbox on the side of the cockpit.

This repeat of the works number only came to light after extensive cleaning of the busbar.

All the available control settings that could be found were then logged together with any other points of special interest. Any remaining areas of paint were also recorded at this stage. The work team then removed all the detachable items from the cockpit, switches, bomb arming panels, control levers and all that remained of the control column which had been found in two halves, the top half and stem being in good condition, the base part having rotted away being formed from an electron magnesium casting. This had been located hanging from the control wires, the bottom bracket having been eroded away by the sea.

The rudder bar was removed next, being in good condition, followed by the fuel priming tank and the oxygen equipment. The oil tank was still "in situ" and was removed. Both port and starboard wings were then separated from the fuselage, and the undercarriage gear removed from the wing torsion box.

All parts were then treated with immersion in a very large tankful of oil to prevent further corrosion. This action proved to be of great value in "buying time" and enabled the group to concentrate on the aluminium parts of the aircraft. At this point of the operation, over 60 hours had been spent collectively by members in the operation of cleaning up and separating the respective parts.

The second work stage marked the start of a five-year reconstruction programme. David Buchanan had hoped that it would not be necessary to strip the whole airframe and that a good museum exhibit could be made by simply replacing the aluminium panels that formed the outer skin where bad corrosion damage was evident, but it became obvious to the group that, after the removal from the sea, the rate of corrosion was now speeding up, despite the initial efforts to contain it. After a few weeks, the whole of the structure was creeping with the pressure of the corrosion build-up between the riveted joints. Large swellings began to form on the panels in the joint areas which grew larger and larger until they burst the riveting apart.

David said that the power of the corrosion spread was extraordinary in the area of the joints; even heavy gauge aluminium, where it was supported by steel sections, suffered, with the steel members being slowly bent under the pressure build up. Naturally members were very alarmed at this sudden increase of destructive forces acting on the wreckage, and they were faced with making an immediate decision on one of two choices: – First, to let the airframe become a total loss or, secondly, to strip the entire airframe down to the last rivet, remove all corrosion and then rebuild, keeping as much of the original airframe as possible.

The position of the museum team was almost identical to the one faced by Jess Henderson's team of divers in 1975 when it seemed that the aircraft could never be brought to the surface and the morale of the group fell to a very low ebb. Museum members felt that if Jess's team could complete their task in the way they did, then they could not let the divers down at this late stage. Naturally a secondary factor on the decision to push ahead was the fact that there were so few examples of Me 109 E4's still around in the world.

Over the years, the museum group had been able to slowly build up a large workshop, and the high cost of obtaining suitable tools had been greatly assisted by donations in the form of an air compressor, an air riveting gun, a complete set of air riveting tools and equipment, all ex-Supermarine. The directors at David's firm had taken a great interest in the specialised work of the museum group and permission was given to use some of the expensive technical metal treatment plant during the work's lunch break.

The group were also very lucky to obtain the voluntary services of a Mr Simon Archibald, an engineer and sheet metal worker who became very interested in the reconstruction of the aircraft.

Armed with this extra help and an enormous amount of optimism, the museum team forged ahead, using the centre section of the airframe as an initial focal point for the work. The Me 109 manual described the centre section as a torque box, because all the airframe stressing originated from the strength of this area. The torque box was totally dismantled and all the rivets were carefully removed by drilling. A special procedure then had to be set up to treat all the aluminium sheet after removal.

First the surface of the sheets were powder honed to re-

112

move all surface and deep-seated corrosion. This system is similar to shot blasting, but involves using a fine glass powder instead, which is far less severe on the metal and makes a good surface for the next process of applying an etch primer. First tests using shot blasting had shown that although quicker in removing the sea fouling and corrosion, it also caused severe "work hardening" of the aluminium sheet, and this would have meant the re-annealing of all the panels before they could be worked again. The next process was to paint the now bright aluminium with an etch primer to the metal and then to apply further coatings of a suitable alkyd paint. The panels were then reassembled and re-riveted back into position on the main spars. Before the reassembly, however, a number of specimen panels were fully treated and subjected to limited outdoor exposure testing. At the time of writing, these panels have not exhibited any signs of breakdown of the surface coating.

To treat the steel members of the airframe, it was necessary to shot blast the metal and then put the members through a special "Blackadising process", a system used at David's place of work. The steel is first dipped into tanks of hot liquid containing salts which are kept running at temperatures of 255° F to 320° F. The dipping process involves six separate tanks. First, there is a degreasing tank, then an acid etching tank, then a tank containing the blacking sources, followed by a neutralising source, and so on. The blacking seems to kill off the penetration into the steel, and the metal emerges with a black matt finish which makes a good surface for a primer coat of paint. The additional surface coatings are then added and the parts thus treated are put back into store until required.

By December, 1977, a progress report on the reconstruction showed that the cockpit floor and frame and the torque box had been completely rebuilt and the group had started the reassembly of many of the main aircraft parts. The main front assembly had been fitted onto a jig ready for the fitting of the outer cockpit runners and side members. All the cockpit side formers had been badly corroded and it had been necessary to remake these items, and thus the next task would be to fit the outer skin.

Naturally a lot of the smaller fittings, like trap nuts and

113

other more general hardware, were unusable and replacements were sought from salvage obtained by the museum group from their work on other ground crashes. This proved to be an excellent supply source for 109 E4 bits and pieces. Another major snag was that all the special castings made from electron aluminium had dissolved in the sea water and the group now faced the task of remaking all these parts by recasting. Curiously all the parts made from ordinary aluminium had been anodised by the aircraft manufacturer and had remained in excellent condition and could all be reused. This, said David, was a splendid advertisement for the quality of the German anodising treatment used during 1939.

One of the major lessons learnt by the group was that there is no quick way around the problem of reconstruction. A tremendous amount of time and energy had to go into the construction of the jigs which had to be exactly right. The jig used for the mounting of the torque box is the outline made for the beaching trolley. Unless the torque box had been properly squared up, it would have been impossible to reassemble the other parts in line and by the time the outer skin was attached the group would have found themselves with bits of unwanted metal which couldn't be lost and tend to look like a tuck in an old jacket pocket.

When they were remaking the side formers, it was necessary to make a reasonably large male former from hardwood shaped to the original. It was difficult because the curve is two directional. On the inside of the former, the rise is almost straight for four inches, but then goes in a long curve with an approximate 4-foot radius. On the outside, the outer part fits close against the wing skin with a much shallower curve. This was found very difficult to reproduce and was achieved by careful shaping of wood. The group then produced a large steel roller for the female part of the former, allowing enough space for the metal to go between the male and female. The roller section was then held in the fork of the workhead of a vertical milling machine where it could turn freely. The male section of the former was then mounted on the worktable of the machine and the aluminium was wound underneath the roller to produce the correct shape. This method worked well. As David put it, "If you try to beat a panel into shape by hand with a hammer, the aluminium deforms and goes into all sorts of odd bumps and shapes."

Some odd facts about the wreckage were felt worthy of recording in the log book. Members working on the dismantling of the fuel injection system of the engine found about half a pint of petrol which had been trapped in the injection pump. When tested the fuel was found to be in good condition after thirty-seven years, and burnt quite readily under test. All the nuts and bolts were removed quite easily after taking out the locking wire and split pins.

The large main attachment wing bolts were pulled out and found to be almost as new. Paradoxically, the electrical gear and rubber cables were in good condition, yet the fuel tank, had disintegrated. Other hoses made from similar rubber remained in good condition. It is still not understood why the tank disintegrated so completely. Perhaps the marine life underwater took a fancy to the taste.

PART TWO

THE BATTLE

October 7, 1940   *Wissant, Northern France*

Lt. Meyer belonged to the second group of the second Staffel of JG51. A German veteran of the Battle of Britain, Meyer made his last flight for the Luftwaffe on October 7, and finished the war as POW in Canada. In 1946 he was repatriated to Western Germany, where he lives at the time of writing. He was located by the museum's German correspondent, Mr Kirchner who taped a long conversation with Meyer about the events of October 7, 1940. The following story is a modified version of the events that took place on that day, seen through the eyes of both German and British pilots.

All of the stories were told from memory by the individuals concerned and without reference to any corroborative documents. All the pilots were concerned that their memories might not be up to the task of total recall. A later chapter records the effect on their stories after certain documents became available to the author.

12 THROUGH GERMAN EYES

Historians record that the dates of the commencement and conclusion of the Battle of Britain were July 1 and the end of October, 1940. Effectively, the Battle had been won by the end of September, and local air superiority over Southern England now rested securely in the hands of the leaders of 10, 11 and 12 Groups of the Royal Air Force. The policy of attacking the Luftwaffe daylight bombers had produced crippling losses in aircraft and aircrew, and the German defensive fighter streams had been unable to fulfil their allotted tactical role. First of the German aircraft to be eliminated from the Battle during July were the JU 87 dive bombers who were massacred by the Spitfires and Hurricanes of Fighter Command. The much vaunted Me 110 had also failed in its role as escort fighter to the bombers, and the Me 109's although a close match for the early marks of Spitfires and Hurricanes, were plagued with the limitations of a short operational range. If the bomb targets were London, then the 109's, based at Wissant, had only one hour and 25 minutes' flying time to complete their sorties. After a climb to 30,000 feet over London, the red fuel warning light would be on in the cockpits, indicating only twenty minutes' flying time left to them. Effectively, this would allow only a few minutes' time for combat, usually at full throttle, and there was a constant dread of having to ditch in the Channel on their return trip.

With the heavy losses experienced by the Do 17 and the He 111 squadrons, new German tactics were developed to allow the bombing of England to continue under cover of darkness. This relieved the Me 109's of their slow, fuel-consuming role as escort fighters, and several units were employed to act as fast fighter-bombers (109 E4's), equipped with 250 kg bombs. Although not to be considered a serious bombing force, the tactic was to escort the fighters with more non-bomb carrying fighters to keep the Fighter Command Spitfires and Hurricanes in the air during the hours of daylight. It had become standard practice for British fighters to concentrate their attacks on the bombers first and then deal with the escorting German fighters. Now the Luftwaffe leaders reasoned that the Me 109 fighter bombers would have to be intercepted and, as they had only one bomb to drop, they could revert to the normal role of interceptor after dropping, which gave them the dual advantage of normal mobility and firepower, not unaaturally, now they were freed from the shackles of escorting the slow moving Dorniers and Heinkels.

October, 1940, heralded the first use of these new tactics. At the same time, some of the Jagdgeschwader units were equipped with the newer Me Bf 109 E7 aircraft. These had certain additional features, both MG and Cannon being fitted, and the M series had two compressors fitted for supercharging against the usual one for the earlier marks. This was said to produce an extra 100/200 hp at the right altitudes.

October 3 and 4 produced rain and drizzle over much of Southern England and German activities were confined mainly to night bombing. On the 5th, a Sunday, weather conditions were still poor, but three squadrons of bomb-carrying 109's attacked West Malling Airfield. Further attacks were made by similar groups during the day at medium to high altitudes, and caused some confusion at 11 Group, the RAF interceptions being ragged and not to maximum effect. On October 6, there was continuous rain over the whole country and little air activity.

*   *   *

October 7, 1940   *Wissant, Northern France*
Lt. Meyer's unit was based in a large meadow bordered by forests on both sides, between Boulogne and Calais. It had the great virtue of being as close to the Channel coast as possible, but suffered the disadvantage of having grass runways, as did many of the German advance airfields used by the Lutfwaffe after Dunkirk.

The meadow was roughly bisected by a road which formed an effective and convenient separation for the three units of JG51. The second Staffel had one side to themselves as they were now operating as fighter bombers under the new orders which had come from no less a person than Kesselring himself.

Meyer's machine, the Me Bf 109 E4, had been equipped with new bomb release gear to carry the single 250 kg bomb, slung between the wheels of the aircraft. Meyer considered this new development as "more propaganda". According to Göring, the Luftwaffe had already destroyed all the Hurricanes and Spitfires that the British possessed; somehow the British hadn't heard about this and, ever since the early days of August, Meyer and his comrades had flown repeated escort missions for the bombers and daily the number of attacking Spitfires and Hurricanes had grown, first attacking the slower He111's and Dorniers, with other squadrons waiting at different levels to harass the escorting fighters. Officially the tactical purpose of the new order was to force the RAF to attack the German fighters. Meyer could not recall any reluctance on their part in the past.

At the briefing, Meyer had heard their commanding officer, Major Werner Mölders, explain the route to their target, "objects of opportunity" on the river banks of the Thames. After the bombs had been dropped by the second Staffel, there was to be a "free hunt" for the British fighters. The first and third Staffels would provide fighter cover on the direct course to London. Werner Mölders would lead the attack from 600 mtrs above the three units, using his radio to keep control of the group, who would be bombing from a height of 6,500 mtrs. The second Staffel was to be led by Victor Mölders, brother of the commanding officer. He had been transferred at his own request from night fighters to JG51 when the previous commanding officer, Hauptmann Wiggers, had been killed on an operation over England. Meyer wondered what Victor Mölders would make of these new tactics. At night, one did not have to worry about Spitfires and Hurricanes, only the flack or, perhaps, one of the slower Blenheims over England. Over Europe, it was the problem of finding the slow-flying Hampdens and Wellingtons of Bomber Command.

Once in the cockpit of his aircraft, Meyer was anxious to

go. The weight of the bomb between the legs of the under-carriage compressed the oleos and made for a harder ride during taxiing over the grass. There was not too much clearance for the belly of the bomb and now, of course, the propeller tips would also be nearer when he lifted the Me's tail during the take-off run.

To add to the hazards, the airfield surface was bumpy and there were nearby high tension wires to consider. Such a take-off was easy for the "Old Eagles", but he knew that some of the new replacements would find their hands full to over-flowing during the first few seconds.

The Me 109 behaved well during take-off. Willie Messer-schmitt had provided his future pilots with a small, cramped cockpit. The L-shaped fuel tank was installed in the fuselage and the lower portion of the L was furnished with a seat. Further back, behind the fuel tank, was a sheet of armour plating, which should protect the pilot from the ravages of bullets and 20 mm cannon fire. There was a second, much smaller piece of armour, placed to protect the rear of the pilot's head. It also served to restrict the view to the vulnerable rear of the aircraft. The pilot normally wore a self-inflating dinghy pack and air bottle, a life jacket and a para-chute. This survival equipment all served to reduce the size of the cockpit and restrict any movement of the pilot's body. When the aircraft was sitting on the ground, the angle of attack of the wings was high, about 17°, and when the 109's were fitted with the newer Daimler Benz 601 engine instead of the less powerful Jumo 210, the first part of the take-off run was almost blind because of the engine bulk. Another penalty of the new engine had been the fitting of 60 lbs of ballast in the tail unit of all aircraft, whose only function was to keep the C/g within limits to compensate for the extra weight up front.

On the Me 109 the cockpit hood did not slide back, thus the pilot could not look out round the edge of the windscreen during take-off. The hood was hinged on the starboard side for entry and exit. Small sliding windows were fitted, one in each panel of the hood. In an emergency, the whole hood and the radio mast could be jettisoned by operation of a special lever which allowed the spring loading of the hood to take effect. Pilots viewed this arrangement with some scepticism, as the departing hood had been known to take part of the tail unit with it, thus depriving the pilot of his control surfaces just when he needed them most on the point of baling out.

The take-off on October 7 was to be without incident. When the signal was given, Meyer opened his slotted flaps to the recommended 20° and checked that the radiator flaps were fully open, and the aircraft trimmed longitudinally slightly nose-heavy. The throttle could be opened very quickly, for the fuel injection system fitted did not choke the engine with rapid throttle opening.

Meyer concentrated on holding the stick hard forward to get the tail up so that he could see where he was going and keep the aircraft straight. He found the acceleration sluggish today, because of the extra weight of the bomb, and the run was much longer than usual. Deliberately he held the aircraft down after flying speed had been gained. Past experience had shown that if the aircraft was pulled off with too little speed, the left wing would not lift, and opposite aileron only produced temporary help by lifting the reluctant wing for a second or two before it dropped again, causing the ailerons to snatch. Small stones flung up from the slipstream of the leading aircraft were, at that moment, striking and abrading the tips of his propeller blades, but he did not feel or even know of their existence. As the aircraft lifted off, Meyer concentrated both on looking for other aircraft of the Staffel and on reducing the drag of his aircraft. He touched the foot-operated wheel brakes before operating the retraction gear of the undercarriage. No point in putting a pair of spinning wheels into the U/C housing. The retraction completed with the sound of two muffled thumps and a slight change of trim, Meyer then fully retracted the flaps and trimmed the aircraft into a climb by operating the two concentric wheels on the left side of the cockpit. The larger hand wheel operated the trim in the "natural" sense (forward for nose heavy) and could be operated by one hand, together with the flap gear wheel.

The Staffel were in loose formation about 100 mtrs apart, and Meyer looked for and found his "squadron hound"*,

* Lutwaffe equivalent of "wingman"

123

Uffz Ludwig, tucked well in position to protect his tail.

Victor Mölders, leading the Staffel, commenced a steady climb on a direct course for the target area without circling to wait for the escorting first and third Staffel of fighters now completing their take-off from the other side of the air field. Unencumbered with bombs, they could easily catch the second Staffel and form in a protective swarm at different levels.

Meyer missed the familiar rush for altitude. The bomb much reduced the rate of climb of the Me 109, which could normally reach the planned operational height of 6,500 mtrs in about six and a half minutes. Time to the target area was to be about 45 minutes from base, and fuel consumption would be heavy.

Passing through the 3,000 mtr level, he began gradually closing the radiator flaps to prevent overcooling of the engine. They passed through broken banks of cumulus cloud and, by now, he could see that the escort fighters were well in position the top layer with Werner Mölders being some 600 mtrs above the second Staffel. By now, Meyer reflected, the RAF fighters would be alerted by their radar operated control rooms, and automatically his eyes began a systematic search of the wide area of sky that could conceal the tiny dots that could grow with such rapidity, filling the large forward panel of his windscreen in a matter of three or four seconds. He cursed the stiffness in his shoulders, brought about by the regular turning of his head to check the sky all around. There was nothing to be seen against the dazzling glare beyond the gentle undulation of the escorting fighters.

By now, Meyer could see the curves of the River Thames ahead and prepared for the order to bomb. He was alerted by the sharp crackle of his radio as Werner Mölders warned of a large formation of Hurricanes to the west. The RAF had already gained a higher position than the German formations, but Mölders, with the special visual facility that seemed to be common to all top fighter pilots, had been the first to see the enemy and report their position. The radio crackled again as Mölders did not react at once to his brother's advice, but led the second Staffel straight toward the formation of Hurricanes for a period of 20 seconds before ordering,

"Make ready". The next 15 seconds seemed to Meyer to drag by until Victor ordered, "Dropping".

Meyer operated his bomb release and felt the sluggishness depart from the controls as the aircraft was relieved of the dead weight. With the rest of his Staffel, he banked for home, but Victor flew a wide climbing turn, together with his wingman. Obviously he wanted to try and spot the impact point of the bombs. "Absolute madness," thought Meyer. "Does he think that he can change the trajectory of the bombs if they are going to miss the target? Doesn't he realise that the dots that were enemy fighters are now diving and growing in size at an appalling rate?" As Meyer watched, the Hurricanes were suddenly behind Victor and his wingman and he could see the hits on both aircraft. Just as suddenly they were both gone.

Meyer and his wingman had turned south to catch up and Meyer was able to see a higher formation of Hurricanes to the east about to dive on the rest of the Staffel. He banked again tightly toward the fighters and watched the wingspan of a Hurricane grow in his reflector gun sight. He squeezed the gun triggers and watched his first short burst go below the belly, now illuminated by the white light of the sun. The Hurricane started a tight turn to starboard and, at the same moment, Meyer felt hits at the rear of his aircraft. He pushed the stick hard away from him, feeling the negative G on his body as the nose of the Me went over the vertical into a steep inverted dive, throttle open against the stop. The ASI went over 400 mph in seconds and Meyer needed all his strength to bring the nose up again.

Looking over his shoulder he saw no sign of his attacker. His airspeed was dropping now as he aileron-turned into thick cloud, levelled off and let the nose rise. The glance behind had been unreassuring. No Hurricane on his tail, but, instead, a white trail of either fuel or coolant fluid spewing out behind from his wing. Already his engine temperature was beginning to rise.

No condensation trail that, but clearly the legacy of bullet strikes in the radiator. He throttled back and, pushing the "transmit" button on the stick, called his wingman.

"Ludwig, I've been hit in the radiator! Fly to the Staffel."

Ludwig did not respond!

*　　*　　*

Flying in the third Staffel, Kurt Müller had an aerial view-point of the attack by the RAF. Flying the newer and faster 109 E7, he nevertheless greatly appreciated the early warning given by Werner Mölders of the higher flying Hurricanes coming in from the west. There was time for the second Staffel to drop their bombs and turn for home, but Victor Mölders seemed to delay the decision to drop for far too long. He saw the bombs drop away and the loose formation break up in the turn for home, with the formation leader and his wingman continuing in a wide climbing turn to watch the bombs' impact. Without any other warning from the radio, Kurt saw that there were other layers of enemy fighters to the east, growing in size in his windscreen at a frightening speed. Then the radio grew alive with warning shouts, and the sky became full of tiny silver shapes. Victor Mölders and his wing-man were the first to be shot down and Müller had a frac-tional glimpse of two Hurricanes attacking Meyer and his wingman from the classic position from below and behind. He saw strikes on both the aircraft and the instant spume of white flowing from the wing radiator of one of them.

From then on he was too occupied in trying to get a Hurricane in his sights to know what happened to that air-craft. All dog-fights were the same. The whirling confusion of high speed shapes which could all look alike, the warning sparkle of tracer, perhaps the vicious thuds of strikes on the armour plate from behind, the violent break away and des-perate visual search for the assassin and the distraction of other aircraft flying at peculiar angles through your reflector gun sight. Just as suddenly, all levels of the sky seemed to empty, leaving only traces of smoke, con-trails and falling wreckage. Then the red-lit tell-tale on the panel reminded him that Wissant was still many minutes' flying time away and that the enemy coast must first be crossed, and then the green water of the Channel. Next – if you were lucky – the landing back at base and the routine of counting in the aircraft. The ground crews and pilots looking at the damage to their machines, the excited exchange of stories in voices far too loud for normality, the hands that shook trying to light the inevitable cigarette. Looking at the machines of the younger "eagles", Kurt wondered how many would be "innocent"* still. This time, losses had been heavy and included two of the flight commanders.

13 THE RAF REPORT

October 7, 1940   *RAF Kenley, Surrey*

P/O Mackenzie of 501 Squadron, 2 Group, was due for an eventful day. RAF Kenley was an old established base situated on the top of the North Downs overlooking the main Eastbourne road. The grass airfield was dry and firm, being well drained, and the buildings and hangars were of pre-war vintage, although now suffering badly from the effects of a heavy raid from Do 217's during August, 1940.

501 Squadron was equipped with Hurricanes fitted with Rotol three-bladed propellers which had variable pitch, a big advance on the old fixed pitch airscrews on the early Hurricane Mk I's. Armament was eight Browning Mgs of 303 calibre, fitted into the wings, which gave the pilots a very lethal cone of fire at about 400 yards. Harmonisation of the guns could be made down to 200 yards, if required, but this distance was usually the subject of much argument amongst pilots, the shorter distance being favoured by those who liked to get really close before opening fire. Those Me 109's fitted with cannon had a certain advantage in range over the Hurricanes, but only some of them were fitted in this way and, as the cannon was fired through the spinner of the propeller, there was rarely time to decide which version was being attacked until hits were made on your aircraft. Performance-wise, the 109's could evade attack from the rear by going into

* The gun muzzles of the Me's were covered with thin rubber cases, not unlike a contraceptive. The term "innocent" grew from those who returned with the covers intact.

a steep dive, the fuel injection engines being untroubled by the negative G forces. The Merlin-engined Hurricanes, having a normal type of carburettor fitted, had to half roll to follow the enemy down.

P/O Mackenzie knew that his Hurricane, which had a strong metal frame with fabric covering, could absorb more punishment than the stressed skin of the Me 109. Certainly the Hurricane had superior manœuvrability both above and below 20,000 feet, but the Me 109 had better speed performance above that height and there was little to choose between the two aircraft below that height.*

On October 7, 1940, 501 Squadron, together with other units from 11 Group, were scrambled and vectored into a mixed raid approaching from the Kent coast. It was a fine clear day, with crisp temperatures, and about 4/8ths cloud cover consisting of convection cumulus between 18 and 22 thousand feet.

The enemy build-up commenced fairly early with a preponderance of 109 bombers and 109 escort at different altitudes for mutual cover, and were spotted by 501 Squadron in the act of dropping their bombs. The interception actually took place in the Maidstone area. P/O Mackenzie recalled that his squadron attacked a medium-sized formation and he saw Sqdn/Ldr Hogan attacking one, while he tried to get his sights on another. He then recalls that Sqdn/Ldr Hogan's Me 109 dived away into a cumulus cloud. Mackenzie reports, "I expected the 109 to do a smart "about-turn" and come out towards me. This had happened a few days previously and I had got a head-on shot at one. However, this one did not do so and I flew through the edge of the cloud and came out some distance behind him. He was streaming glycol, as Hogan had undoubtedly hit his radiator. As he was slowing considerably, I caught up to about 300 yards and gave it a short burst from behind and below – noting strikes on the fuselage and engine. He lost more speed and obviously could not make it back over the Channel, so I broke away and climbed back to re-engage a small flight of 109's."

After reaching a height of 26,000 feet, he attacked from

* *See appendix – RAF wartime report on the handling of the Me 109.*

beneath the formation and was rewarded with the sight of the rear Me 109 doing a half roll and dive in the direction of the English coast near Dover. He dived after the Me 109 and, after firing a three-second burst, could detect the speed of the Me dropping off to about 250 mph. He again positioned himself behind the Me for another attack, but found that he had used up all his ammunition. The Me flew on in a straight line, taking no evasive action at all, so Mackenzie signalled the pilot to land on the water, but the pilot ignored the warning, although still losing height and speed.

By now Mackenzie could just see the French coast, so he came in from the left of the Me and, after positioning his wing above the Me's tailplane, used maximum aileron and forced his wing tip onto the tail of the Me. The stresses proved too much, both for the Hurricane wing tip and the Me tailplane, and about three feet of the Hurricane wing tip departed upward and backward. The Me tail collapsed and the aircraft dived into the sea. Two other Me's then attacked Mackenzie and duly shot up his engine, causing him to make a wheels-up landing after just clearing the Folkestone cliffs. Mackenzie went back to Kenley by surface transport. He was subsequently awarded the DFC for his exploits that day.

* * *

Flt/Lt Holden recalled the interception on October 7 rather differently to P/O Mackenzie. Holden was a veteran of a number of air battles, many of them in France prior to the evacuation of the British Forces. A peace time officer of the RAF since 1936, Holden had been trained to fly on Tiger Moths, graduating to the Hawker Harts, the Fury and then the Gloucester Gauntlet and Gladiator with 56 Squadron. The Squadron had converted to Hawker Hurricanes in 1939 from their base at Martlesham Heath and had been mainly engaged in convoy escort duties. The range of the Hurricane was about 1 hour 20 minutes, depending on how you used your engine. There was a great deal of difference in cruising and +4 boost operation.

Early in 1940, Ft/Lt Holden was posted to 501 Squadron based at Tangmere and, when the Germans invaded France and the Low Countries, the Squadron went to France in a

129

great hurry and were very soon struggling for survival in a situation where there was no fixed front line and air superiority was clearly in the hands of the Luftwaffe.

Holden recalled that he was shot down on his third day in France and made a forced landing with the cockpit of his Hurricane full of smoke and fumes. In six weeks the squadron had lost twenty-nine pilots and fifty-six aircraft. The squadron returned to the UK on June 19 for regrouping and re-equipping at Tangmere. He remembered the names of four of the pilots who returned with him. They were Brian Cridland, Ken Boothroyd, Kenneth Lee and Ginger Lacey.

At this time, the squadron acquired a new C/O, S/Ldr Harry Hogan, who soon got the unit, now based at Croydon, hard at practice flights and night flying in preparation for the forthcoming Battle of Britain, which had to be the obvious prelude to the German invasion of the UK.

After a week at Croydon, the squadron moved to Kenley, and Flt/Lt Holden recalled that some members of 501 Squadron had tea with the King (then George VI). He said that it was a totally unofficial visit, the King arriving with Basil Embry (AVM). S/Ldr Hogan and Holden were present and, though there was no reason given for the Royal visit, Flt/Lt Holden thought that he just wanted to talk to the pilots who had been in France to understand the conditions that prevailed at the time.

During the first few weeks of the Battle of Britain, Holden had to go into hospital for an operation and, when he rejoined 501, there was a great deal of activity in the air. He said, "Every day we were charging about somewhere." Later on, his log book showed that October was a little quieter, the unit being airborne on the 2nd (twice), the 4th (three times) and twice on the 7th. He said that by the beginning of October the RAF were definitely on top, as the Germans had previously suffered very heavy losses. He thought that the tactic of using fighter bombers began around October, and it was currently thought that the bomb-carrying Me 109's carried no armament and could only climb up to about 23,000 feet.

On October 7, 1940, 501 Squadron was scrambled from Kenley onto some bomb-carrying Me 109's and their escort. Flt/Lt Holden was leading the squadron that day. When he spotted the Me 109's they had just dropped their bombs and appeared to be flying back south to base, but at the same height as the Hurricanes (21,000 feet). Holden ordered his unit into line astern and he attacked the first one, "fair and square". This shot gave him special gratification as he was turning onto the tail of the Me firing as he did so. The Me was flying very steadily and took no evasive action. Holden went on to say that he suspected that his first burst had killed the pilot, as he started to turn lazily to the right (seen from behind) and Holden last saw him in a near vertical dive. He was sure that he had killed the pilot as the behaviour of the aircraft was abnormal and, with experience, you could usually tell, as the dead pilot continues to feed onto the controls for a moment or two and, as he flops, the aircraft usually turns one way or the other. The engagement took only a matter of seconds and he did not see any glycol streaming away from the wing of the Me.

When chasing a second Me 109 toward the south coast, he got in a good burst and certainly hit the aircraft, but it shot off in a steep dive into cloud with Holden chasing hard. Holden said that his windscreen misted up and although he continued the dive, he did not see that particular aircraft again. He was most careful to stress that the engagement was over in a matter of seconds.

Flt/Lt Holden said that P/O Mackenzie was not in his section. He would have been able to go in from another angle. He added, "Mac was a very good pilot."

Flt/Lt Holden survived the war, retiring from the RAF in 1964 with the rank of Wing Commander.*

* * *

The C/O of 501 Sqdn remembered the day differently to the others. He was S/Ldr C. A. V. Hogan (Now Air Vice Marshal Hogan) and he recalls flying on two sorties. Unfortunately he was unclear of the times of the sorties.

His log book showed that on the second patrol of the day 7 October, 1940, the Squadron was on patrol in the Ashford–West Malling area and S/Ldr Hogan recalled that they were vectored onto a formation of Me 109's. When the Squadron attacked, having the advantage of height, the Me 109's dropped

* See appendix

their bombs indiscriminately and turned for home. He attacked one of a group of seven Me's at close range. He went on to say that P/O Mackenzie was probably flying as his No. 2 and he attacked the same aircraft after the S/Ldr overran it. He also thought that both he and Mackenzie were given a half share of one Me 109 destroyed. He was flying Hurricane No. 7229 on that day.

14 THE LAST MOMENTS OF FLIGHT

Lt Meyer knew that his future flying time was strictly limited. The engine was beginning to overheat and he throttled back to try and save it for as long as possible to stretch his flight home. Without his wingman to protect his rear, his position was vulnerable to enemy attack. With other aircraft still in sight, he decided to fox the enemy. He pulled the stick gently back, his forward speed dropping off rapidly. With 110 mph on the clock, he felt the wing slots open and the onset of aileron snatch. With little slipstream from the propeller, the Me became rather unsteady near the stall and at 83 mph buffeting commenced and lateral control became critical. A good bootfull of rudder and the aircraft commenced the spin.

Meyer watched his altitude with care and, after six turns of the spin, he eased the stick forward and centralised the rudder. With its usual low speed docility, the aircraft came out of the spin. He opened the throttle and headed into a gentle turn to cross the coast between Dover and Dungeness, thus avoiding the flack concentrated on the Dover area. By using short bursts of engine he was able to maintain an altitude of 1,200 mtrs but the engine temperature still rose too fast. The cockpit was becoming hot and an ominous smell of burning oil warned of an impending fire risk. Height was falling off rapidly and, quite suddenly, the airframe shook with a series of jerks and the propeller stopped. Meyer checked his height. With 400 mtrs left, there was no chance of crossing the Channel. The coastline at Dymchurch passed below and

Meyer was very tempted to make a landing on the beach. He tried the radio again, saying, "I am hit in the radiator and am ditching in the Channel – Es liebe Deutschland!"

The act of ditching an aircraft is usually a 'first-time' operation for most pilots. The most important factor is certainly the state of the sea. Meyer's luck was in, as the wave motion was small, the wind being light in the region of eight knots. He elected to land into wind toward the wave motion. He first ejected the cockpit canopy safely, then selected full flap (42.5°), checked that the undercarriage was up and locked, keeping the aircraft in a gentle glide at an indicated 90 mph. With the cabin cover gone, he could look over the side of the aircraft and select his ditching area at leisure in a wide gliding turn. The leading edge slots were already open. The strong smell of burning dispersed rapidly with the open cockpit, and Meyer loosened the snap of his helmet, disconnected his throat microphone and headphones, and flew as slowly as possible over the water. When very low, he turned the landing flaps into the "up" position to prevent the water entering the flap recesses in the wings in the hope of keeping afloat a little longer. Now, at sea level, he lifted the nose slightly and almost at the same time the belly of the Me skimmed the surface. Then came a series of three shocks as the airframe 'became water-borne and decelerated rapidly. The last shock was violent as the bulky nose dug into the water, re-emerging slowly and shipping sea into the cockpit.

Now Meyer had to act quickly. He unfastened his safety harness, then undid the parachute harness and, standing on the aircraft seat, he took a header into the water and swam from the Me 109 as quickly as possible. When he was twenty feet away, he opened the valve of the small air bottle of his life jacket, then the valve of his dinghy, which inflated rapidly, leaving him only the problem of climbing aboard. This completed with some difficulty, he just had enough time left to watch the Messerschmitt sink slowly out of sight, going down nose first. The cold of the sea water was beginning to make itself felt and he wondered if his ditching had been spotted from the coast. Initially he had the mad idea of waiting in the water till it was dark and then hand paddling the odd mile or so to the shore. Once ashore, perhaps he could find some drift wood or wreckage to use as oars and row himself back to

France. Or perhaps the "Seenotflugkommando" would have been alerted by his comrades and would already be on their way to save him from the shore batteries of the British.

Both were forlorn hopes. His radio had been put out of action by the same burst of gunfire that had damaged his radiator, and he was too far from the shore to see the anti-invasion scaffold poles and miles of barbed wire with anti-personnel mines that would prevent his access to the high water mark to gather his drift-wood.

As Meyer sat in his dinghy, he reflected that his beloved Messerschmitt had sunk in about twenty seconds. Others of his Staffel who had ditched and survived had always said that the Messerschmitt made a bad boat. He searched the horizon and the shore line, looking vainly for help. As he did so, he spotted another aircraft, gliding down to the sea about 500 mtrs to his West. He was almost certain that it was another Messerschmitt 109, and wondered if it was his wingman, Uffz Ludwig.

It was *two hours* before Meyer saw another aircraft, this time a Lysander observation 'plane from the RAF. It came from the direction of Dover and, spotting his dinghy, did a 180° turn, came low over the water and dropped a smoke flare to mark his position. The aircraft then flew on out to sea.

About twenty minutes later two small coastal patrol vessels arrived and a rope ladder was thrown down to him from the deck of one of them. When he had managed to climb up on deck, he was taken to a cabin. By now the cold had enveloped him and he remembered taking off his soaked clothing and climbing into a bunk bed, and blankets being wrapped round him to ward off the cold and the longer term effects of shock. He slept almost instantly and awoke to find the boat engines had stopped. Someone told him that they were in Dover Harbour.

*   *   *

Lt Meyer was arrested and taken to a cell in the nearby barracks for formal interrogation. He was then passed to a transit camp and taken by road to a POW camp at Hyde Park in London. Here he met some other German pilots and was taken with them to another camp, which he thought was named "Cockforest" (?Cockfosters). After more detailed interrogation, he was taken with another group of Luftwaffe officers to what he described as "a close custody POW camp". It was a castle called Grisedale Hall and had all the barbed wire trimmings with corner watch towers and searchlights. One of his colleagues, a Lt von Werra, escaped and tried to steal a Hurricane from a nearby RAF airfield, but was caught before his scheme came to fruition.

In 1941 Meyer was sent to Canada, remaining there until the summer of 1946, when he was repatriated to Delemhorst, Germany.

15 ET TU BRUTE

"It isn't really blind flying, the instruments aren't in braille."
(Tee Emm)

So who did shoot down Lt Meyer? Historian F. K. Mason said that it was Flt/Lt Holden. One of the main difficulties in comparing the British combat reports was that there were two Me 109 fighter bomber raids on London that day, one at about 10.15 a.m. and the second at 1.15 p.m. Meyer could not recall with certainty the time of the raid on October 7.

Further confusion is added by a passage taken from a book written by Werner Mölders, "Mölders und seine Manner". Here the bombing raid (October 7, 1940) is written from Werner Mölders' higher viewpoint. He said, "Well, I myself took part. He (talking about his brother, Victor Mölders) was so careless, the boy was on a flight to England to drop bombs. All the pilots had dropped their bombs over London without attack against us. Whilst the others were flying home, Victor was making a wide turn to watch the impact of the bombs − a quite useless matter. Suddenly, the Hurricanes were behind him and Lt Meyer and they must have been shot down."

In Meyer's report, he said, "I, the Staffel leader, flew with my 'squadron hound', Uffz Ludwig, in the Staffel. NOT as escort to Victor Mölders." So again, we have a contradiction of evidence from the German side. In a letter to the author, Francis K. Mason (author of "Battle over Britain") said that he felt that the battle situation on October 7 could have been complicated by the appearance of some of the members of the Polish 303 Squadron, who claimed to have taken part in the dog-fight against JG51. He goes on to say: "The difficulty with most of the Battle of Britain was that for every German aircraft known to have been shot down, there were, on average, 3.4 combat reports filed claiming its destruction. It is only by using a computer that one can arrive at the degree of probability that one or two particular pilots did, in fact, destroy a particular aircraft (German). To this must be added such details that one could get from the travelling form 700, which sometimes recorded the amount of ammunition expended on a sortie." He adds: "The aircraft shot down by Mackenzie was unquestionably an aircraft of JG27 and was flying about four miles away from the position of the combat involving JG51. There is also a slight discrepancy in time which tallies with German records."

As Mackenzie claims to have got in a burst at Meyer's aircraft and then climbing back to intercept the returning bombers before making his second and successful attack on another Me 109 (the wing tipping incident), one wonders if that last aircraft was the one that F. K. Mason was referring to as belonging to JG27, always assuming that Lt Meyer was flying on the 10 a.m. sortie and not the 1.15 p.m. sortie.

As the early Victorian novelists used to say: – "The plot thickens!"

In Flt/Lt Holden's interview with the author, he is certain that he led 501 Squadron on October 7 in the 10.15 a.m. interception of JG51. He is also certain that the Me 109 he attacked had just dropped its bomb and was heading for home. He is equally certain that he killed the pilot with his first burst. If Holden was right, then he could not have attacked Meyer in his first assault. So who did he shoot down? Victor Mölders or his wingman? In his first attack, both were shot down.

In Holden's second attack, he was well on the way to the south coast and, in a separate letter to the author, he said, "All I remember of that encounter is that I got off a good

136

burst at him and certainly hit him, but he shot off in a steep dive with me after him. My bullet-proof windscreen fogged up, which nearly drove me mad and, although I charged on, I was unable to see enough to find him again. Of course, it was all in a matter of seconds of time. However, it is very feasible to suppose that he had to do a controlled landing in the sea."

It must be remembered that Flt/Lt Holden was, by this time, a very experienced fighter pilot. He had been credited with victories in France prior to the Battle of Britain, and had also been shot down himself. His powers of observation and skills as a fighter pilot were at their peak and he would not, as a matter of principle, make a claim for a combat in which he could not produce conclusive evidence of destruction.

By contrast, P/O Mackenzie was inexperienced, having just commenced his career as a fighter pilot, but he, too, was to develop into a courageous and dangerous opponent for the Luftwaffe. In his encounter with an Me 109 trailing vapour from its wing radiator on October 7, he claimed to have scored hits on the engine and fuselage. The aircraft slowed down considerably and Mackenzie said, "He lost so much speed, I knew he couldn't make it back over the Channel, so I climbed back to re-engage the raid."

Meyer does not mention a second attack. Additionally, there were only four identifiable bullet holes in the parts of his aircraft recovered from the sea. Again, the ravages of thirty-seven years underwater may have turned bullet holes into unidentifiable sea damage. Meyer was also very pre-occupied with smoke and fumes in his cockpit, together with a failing engine and the imminent prospect of ditching in enemy waters, and might not have noticed the second attack. If this sounds too unlikely, remember that when an engine seizes up in flight, it does so with a series of jerks that nearly rip it out of the airframe and the pilot would be very occupied with the control of his machine.

Perhaps Meyer's remark, "I, the Staffel leader, flew with my 'squadron hound', Uffz Ludwig, in the Staffel, NOT as escort to Victor Mölders", gives us a better clue to the German order of battle that day. If he flew in two sorties on October 7, perhaps his memory over a thirty-seven-year interval has confused the two raids. Why was he leading the Staffel? Was it because the Staffel leader, Victor Mölders, was shot down on the first raid, and Meyer, as senior pilot, took his place on the second raid?

If this theory is right, then Meyer's combat report contradicts itself in several places. Unfortunately it also contradicts the report by Kurt Müller, who records the shooting down of both Mölders, and Meyer in the same raid. If he, too, has confused the two raids, perhaps it was because the Staffel lost two leaders on that day – a very serious matter for the morale of the group.

16 HUMAN MEMORY AND THE TIME FACTOR

In the writing of this book, the research for the British pilot's stories had coincided with the closure of the relevant files at the public records office, because of the opening of a new records office at Kew, London, at the end of October, 1977.

At first, all contact with the British pilots was made by letter and later by tape-recordings. The only aide-memoir to bridge the span of thirty-seven years was the pilot's individual log book which only recorded the barest minimum detail; e.g. the date, the aircraft flown, any E/A shot down and possibly the patrol area. W/C Mackenzie lost his log book in 1946, so he didn't even have this memory jogger.

During November, 1977, details of 501 Squadron operational reports again became available for research, and copies of the operational combat reports for October 7, 1940, were read by the museum researchers with some confusion.

The timing of the raid by the Me 109 fighter bombers could have been either at 10.15 hours or 13.00 hours, or even both times. Neither Eric Meyer or Kurt Müller were certain of the timing, but both German pilots were sure of the date: October 7, 1940.

Current thinking by air historians had recorded that Meyer was shot down by F/Lt Holden (F. K. Mason) at 10.30 hours, or, alternatively, at 13.15 hours by S/Ldr Hogan and

138

P/O Mackenzie (air historian Peter Cornwell). 501's combat reports revealed a different story.

The 10.15 hours raid on London

F/Lt Holden led the Squadron flying as Blue 1, B Flight. He said, "In company with 501 Squadron, I turned onto five Me 109's flying at 24,000 feet North West of Ashford."

He goes on: "I then saw three 109's on my right and attached myself to one of these aircraft and, thinking that he was flying faster, opened fire at 400 yards with an eight second burst, without result. As I began to catch him up at 300 yards, I gave him a second burst with some effect as smoke belched out. At 2,000 feet he passed over the coast as I closed with him and fired off the rest of my ammunition and saw him dive into the sea off Dungeness."

His combat report claimed one Me 109 destroyed. To the museum researchers the report had nothing to link it with Meyer's story except the date and place. Sadly, Holden's story didn't sound much like his earlier tape-recording to the author.

However, looking further into F/Lt Holden's combat reports for October, 1940, it was found that on October 12, 1940, he claimed an Me 109 destroyed over Robertsbridge in Kent. In this report he attacked an aircraft (Me 109) at 23,000 feet, which then dived vertically for several thousand feet. On his second attack he saw glycol stream away from the wing radiator. He attacked again and saw bits fly off the E/A and oily black smoke pouring out. Holden said that his windscreen was obscured and he lost sight of the aircraft.

Sgt Lacey of 501 Squadron reported seeing a Me 109 diving into the sea between Dungeness and Beachy Head at this time.

This report sounded much more akin to F/Lt Holden's taped version. On October 25, 1940, F/Lt Holden, again flying as Blue leader, made two attacks on Me 109's near Hawkinge in Kent. On his second attack at close range, he saw bits fly off the aircraft and both radiators streamed glycol. He did not claim to have seen the aircraft ditch.

Busy as ever, F/Lt Holden claimed an Me 109 damaged on October 26, 1940, at 12.15 hours off Hastings. He saw strikes on the aircraft and glycol coming from the radiator, but he lost the aircraft in cloud at 8,000 feet.

It was at this point that the museum researchers realised that Holden's first report had combined some of the incidents in these four October combat reports into one story. Many of the details were the same, but only the time factor had telescoped the events. The question that the researchers now had to ask was, "Would all the other pilots have similar time changes in their memories of past events?"

Now, a squadron combat report is written by the pilot, usually on the same day as the events recorded. It is generally very brief and refers to details about the claim for an aircraft shot down or damaged. In no way can it be thought of as anything but a claim. Other pilots from different squadrons in the same area and at the same time make similar claims and it is up to those monitoring all the reports to decide from the evidence offered who shot down or shared in the shooting down of any particular enemy aircraft.

Initially the monitoring of the reports is done by the squadron intelligence officer. The reports are then forwarded to the RAF Group commanding a number of squadrons. In the case of 501 Squadron, they were part of 11 Group of Fighter Command.

The 13.15 hours raid on London Docks

P/O Mackenzie's combat report for the 7 October, 1940, claimed two Me's destroyed (one shared) and that he was flying as Blue 4 in B Flight. The attacks were made at *13.15* and *13.40* respectively. The two attacks were made at 6,000 feet and 23,000 feet respectively. He said: "When on patrol with 501 Squadron, between Ashford and West Malling at 23,000 feet, I followed Red 1 (Sqdn/Ldr Hogan) in attacking a Me 109. Red 1 damaged the glycol tank of the E/A, which dived into cloud at 5,000 feet. I flew above Red 1 above the cloud bank and the E/A came out of the cloud bank at 5,000 feet, at right angles to his previous flight path. I dived and attacked him from astern at 250 yards range. He lost height and went into the sea off Hythe.

"The aircraft sank slowly, the tail being visible for some

time. I then climbed back to 23,000 feet and continued to patrol Dover/Folkestone . . . when I saw eight Me 109's coming across my line of flight."

(The report then goes on to describe the encounter narrated in Chapter 13 which resulted in the wing busting incident and the subsequent forced landing near Folkestone.)

This report was of considerable interest to the museum researchers and, checking back against the four letters written by Mackenzie, it seemed that the events closely matched those taken from Lt Meyer's report.

Was there a time lag problem for Mackenzie? The short answer was yes. In his first letter, he mentioned the attack as being in the company of Sqdn/Ldr Hogan. By the time he wrote again he had looked up some old records (Mason's book?) and thought that the attack might have been made jointly with F/Lt Holden. In the same letter he thought that the attack commenced around 10.15 hours on October 7 (as quoted by Mason). So, having mentally established the time link, he resolutely refused to be diverted from the new time scale in his later letters. To try and trigger his mind back to his original time, the museum researchers noticed that one newspaper report of his doings on the 7 October stated that, when he crash landed, he hit his face on the gun sight in the Hurricane. If this had happened on the 10.15 hours patrol after a crash landing, it seemed logical to suppose that he would have had medical attention at Folkestone before returning to his unit at Kenley by car. There just could not have been time for him to have got back to his unit and take part in the 13.15 hours interception. *Ergo*, he must have flown on the later patrol that day in the first place. This point was put to him by the museum researchers and it really misfired.

Mackenzie wrote back to say that the forced landing knocked his chin on the reflector sight and cut through the gums, breaking the roots of four of his teeth, the cut being sewn up by a service doctor at Folkestone. He went back to Kenley by car and was off operations for five days, so he couldn't have been on the afternoon interception. Yet his combat report, duly signed by him, said that his combat had been at 13.15 on October 7, 1940. Apart from this time lapse, the details contained in his letters almost exactly matched the events of 1940 and, of all the pilots interviewed, his total recall of events was the most detailed.

So, who was Mackenzie flying with on the 13.15 patrol, and who got in the first burst at Meyer? The logical answer seemed to be Sqdn/Ldr Hogan, the C/O of 501 Squadron. He was located living in Hertfordshire, now retired from the RAF with the rank of Air Vice Marshal. In his letters to the museum he said that his records showed he had been airborne twice on October 7, 1940, and on the second patrol of the day in the area of West Malling/Ashford they attacked seven Me 109's. He went on to say that his log entry mentioned sharing the destruction of an Me 109 with Mackenzie, adding that he also remembered recommending Mackenzie for the immediate award of the DFC. He was not sure if it was for that particular mission. He also said that F/Lt Holden would have probably flown both patrols on that day. To help in the search, he mentioned that the squadron would have put up about twelve aircraft on that day. He could remember the names of some of the pilots, which included Ginger Lacey, Farnes, Haris, Whitehouse, Morfill and Lea. The point was, had any of these gallant gentlemen also made out combat reports for October 7?

Back at the records office at Kew, museum researchers found that Sqdn/Ldr Hogan's memory of events had been very good. His combat report was for the second patrol of the day, timed at 13.15 hours. He was flying Red 1, A Flight, and the report claimed a 109 (shared) destroyed. The narrative said, "I attacked one from astern until it commenced a dive toward cloud at 2,000 feet. I followed, firing off the rest of my ammunition. At one point, a thick stream of glycol came away from the aircraft, but that seemed to stop after about eight seconds. I think some bits also came off it. The Me 109 went into cloud over Ham St. and evaded me on the turn."

He added, cryptically, "This was due to finding another Hurricane in the cloud." He concluded with the words, "I went on below cloud but did not see the Me 109 again."

To researchers, this sounded very like the attack that Meyer had described, but the height of the cloud was wrong. Mackenzie said 5,000 feet, Hogan said he was diving toward 2,000 feet; but Mackenzie was watching and could perhaps

142

spare the time to check his altimeter, whereas Hogan was actually trying to get his sights on the Me 109 and probably guessed at the height when making out the report.

Hogan's report commenced with the words "I was leading 501 Squadron on patrol over Sevenoaks in company with 605 Squadron." This statement put 605 Squadron in the right place and the right time to also intercept the 13.15 hours raid. To get a better picture of the battle, researchers now had to check all 605 Squadron's combat reports for October 7. Would there be claims from these pilots that could point in the direction of Meyer's demise?

Before checking, it was noteworthy that Sgt Ginger Lacey of 501 Squadron had also filed a combat report for October 7. He was flying Yellow 2 on the 13.15 patrol and claimed an Me 109 as a "probable". He was patrolling at 25,000 feet in the Ashford area, and saw five Me 109's diving down to attack.

He said, "I turned behind the rear E/A and opened fire at 150 yards, and saw glycol coming from his centre radiator (!). The aircraft went into a vertical dive, rotating to the right. I did not see that aircraft again."

Researchers jumped hard at the mention of a centre radiator. The 109 4B had two underwing radiators, and it seemed likely that Lacey had either opened fire on a Hurricane or had mistaken the Me's centre bomb rack for a radiator, and the vapour seen could have been petrol as the fuel tank was directly above the rack. If this was the case, then this Me 109 could have well been the second Me to ditch near Dungeness when Meyer was in his dinghy. Only a few minutes separated the ditching of the two aircraft, and there could not have been much fuel left in the tanks of any of the Me 109's at this stage of the operation.

A hard look at the combat reports of 605 Squadron provided this additional information:—

The 10.15 hours raid: 605 Squadron

Sqdn/Ldr McKeller of 605 Squadron reported, "I was leading 'Turkey' Squadron at 27,000 feet above 501 Squadron near Maidstone, and, after several vectors, control reported

'Bandits' to the North East. 501 Squadron turned west along the south bank of the river and we saw AA bursts. I kept the Squadron to the South and in the sun and we saw seven E/A's Me 109's approaching and going South East. I ordered individual attacks and following one I opened fire at 300 yards, seeing hits and dense white smoke from the radiator of an Me 109. The aircraft started to draw away and then commenced to emit black smoke as well. (Indicating an overheating engine.) I last saw him South East of Dungeness. I landed back at base (Croydon) at 11.00 hours." Sqdn/Ldr McKeller claimed one Me 109 damaged.

To the researchers, the sky over Kent both at 10.15 hours and 13.30 hours appeared to be rapidly filling up with aircraft with glycol streaming from their radiators. More incidents were to be reported.

The combat report from Sgt Wright of 605 Squadron claimed one Me 109 damaged. Flying as Yellow 1, A Flight of 605 Squadron at 10.15 hours on October 7, 1940, he said, "Yellow section were airborne at 09.40 hours and on patrol with 501 Squadron in the South London/Maidstone area. We sighted seven Me 109's flying East at 25,000 feet and as we were at 1,000 feet above them, we dived down to attack.

"Three 109's passed below me, and I got in a two second burst at one from his stern quarter. He then dived and I gave chase and positioned myself underneath him where he couldn't see me. I got to 150 yards range and then fired a seven second burst seeing some smoke coming from the top of the engine cowling, as he tried to climb away. I held my position and the smoke stopped. I then fired the rest of my ammunition at him and saw glycol coming from his wing radiator. I left him five miles South East of Maidstone slowly losing height."

At this point, researchers reached slowly for the brandy bottle to get a suitable reserve of fuel on board before becoming totally submerged in a welter of combat reports. Turning back the pages of history requires accurate data on which to base a museum story. The vital question was, how do you eliminate individual reports unless the pilot concerned actually saw the E/A crash.

During the Battle of Britain, it was considered highly dangerous to follow down after damaging an enemy aircraft.

144

The victor would naturally concentrate his attention on the victim and leave his own tail wide open for attack.

The next report made by P/O Muirhead of 605 Squadron for the 10.15 hours raid emphasised the dangers of getting too involved in watching a potential victim.

Flying as Blue 17 of B Flight, he saw seven Me 109's approaching about 1,000 feet below heading South East. He attacked the leading aircraft from the stern quarter, firing a four second burst at 200 yards range. He then saw the E/A slow down and observed that his strikes had been effective as pieces began to come rapidly adrift from the damaged aircraft. As he watched, his aircraft was mortally hit from behind and an explosion occurred, sending the Hurricane into a spin from which recovery proved impossible as the rudder controls had been severed. P/O Muirhead then said that he waited until he was low enough to undo his oxygen tube, and he left his aircraft at 4,000 feet in cloud, landing in a wood near Dartford. His aircraft was burnt out.

The 13.15 hours raid (605 Squadron combat reports)

Here the C/O, Sqdn/Ldr McKeller, provided researchers with some very positive information about the interception. As usual, he was flying as Red 1, A Flight, and reported engagements with Me 109's between 13.20 and 13.40 hours in the Westerham/Maidstone area. He claimed four Me 109's destroyed – a remarkable feat of airmanship.

He said: "Leading 'Turkey' Squadron and following 501 Squadron, we were attacked by Spitfires (Code letter LZ/P) while patrolling Sevenoaks." (Fortunately, the mistake was discovered before anyone got hurt, although McKeller's recommendation that the pilots concerned should be allowed to visit a Hurricane squadron and actually look at one on the ground seemed a fairly mild sarcasm compared with what he probably said over the R/T at the time.)

After this mix-up, McKeller said, "Shortly after we were told to patrol base. Control then reported E/A at 15,000 to 25,000 feet in the Biggin Hill area.

"I spotted fifteen Me 109's being followed by 50+E/A at various heights. We did a No. 1 attack and saw a bomb being dropped by a Me 109 which I attacked. Pieces flew off the aircraft, which then went into an outside spin, emitting dense white smoke and vapours." (This aircraft was observed to crash in a field north of the railway Brasted/Westerham area by Sgt Jones.)

McKeller then attacked a second Me 109 which immediately burst into flames and went down inverted East of Biggin Hill. He was attacked in turn by a 109, which he lost after a brief fight. He then descended to 15,000 feet and found Me's all over the sky and all heading South East. He said: "I attacked one from astern and hit his radiator. White vapour came out and fogged up my windscreen. (How close can you get?) I attacked him a second time and he burst into flames and crashed into a wood near a quarry, West of Maidstone."

McKeller then attacked a fourth Me 109 from astern and the aircraft caught fire and the pilot baled out. The aircraft crashed North of the railway line between Ashford and Tonbridge. He landed back at base, out of ammunition at 14.10 hours.

Not unnaturally, researchers took a hard look at McKeller's report. It was the first "combat report" to mention that the 109's were actually dropping bombs, although W/C Mackenzie, W/C Holden and AVM Hogan all recalled in their letters that the interceptions were on Me 109's that were dropping, or had dropped, their bombs.

McKeller's first combat sounded interesting in respect of the dense white fumes and the subsequent spin. McKeller did not see the aircraft crash although it was claimed to have been observed by Sgt Jones of 605 Squadron, which presupposes the thought that Sgt Jones did follow it down from 25,000 feet. He could, of course, have been at a much lower altitude and sighted the demise of another enemy aircraft. McKeller also mentioned that the Me 109 was in an outside spin (with the cockpit on the outside of the spin instead of the inside, as was more usual). Meyer's spin was of the "inside" variety, so researchers reluctantly concluded it could not have been his aircraft. None of the other attacks made by McKeller could have been Meyer, as they were all victims that went down in flames.

The only other combat report from a member of 605

146

Squadron for the 13.15 hours raid came from P/O D. Ford, flying as Blue 2 of B Flight. He claimed a Me 109 damaged at a height of 5,000 feet South East of Sevenoaks. He said:

"When on patrol in the Biggin Hill area at 25,000 feet, we attacked a formation of Me 109's in line astern. We were then attacked by another formation. I chased three 109's diving South East for the coast. I fired a three second burst and obtained some hits. I then closed behind him and gave a 5/6 second burst and the E/A dived away into cloud emitting smoke. My windscreen iced up and I lost him, but on emerging from cloud I saw a large fire in a wood at Seal Chart, South East of Sevenoaks."

The records do not show if this fire was, in fact, caused by an aircraft crashing.

So far as museum researchers could tell, these reports for the two raids (10.15 and 13.15 hours) provided the only evidence now available of who shot down Meyer. The next thing to be straightened out was the German side of the story. Did JG 51 take part in both raids, and on which raid was Lt Meyer shot down? Secondly, who picked up Meyer after the ditching?

As the Royal Lifeboat Institution did not record Meyer's pick-up, perhaps the records office could provide details about air/sea rescue units operating in the area on October 7. Here researchers drew a complete blank.

No. 27 A/S Rescue unit was operating in the Ramsgate/Dover area, but its operational records did not record any pick-up during October.

No. 28 A/S Rescue unit was formed at Newhaven on 22.7.40 but, again, there was no recorded information during October, 1940.

No. 29 A/S Rescue unit was well to the west of the area at Littlehampton, and had nothing to report for the Hythe area for October.

No. 30 A/S Rescue unit was based at Calshott and formed in 1939. They were too far West to be involved.

No. 31 A/S Rescue unit was nearer at Sheerness but had been formed too late in 1942 to have been involved.

No. 32 A/S Rescue unit was formed in 1944 and was thus well out of the running on a time basis alone.

It was clear that sea pick-ups were made by other ships at

the time of the October 7 raid, and understandably left only small Royal Navy craft or fishing boats available to do the job. However, the Lysander aircraft that Meyer saw, certainly spotted him and reported his position. It was possible that the aircraft came from RAF Station Hawkinge or RAF Station Manston, both units being close to the final pick-up area.

In direct contrast to the RAF, the Luftwaffe had its own special organisation for the rescue of crashed aircrew which had been formed years before the outbreak of war. With considerable forethought, these units were equipped with Dornier flying boats, and Heinkel seaplanes and were used in conjunction with fast motor launches, which provided a back-up service or were used when the sea was too rough for aircraft to land. Additionally, a number of specially prepared rescue floats were built and sited in mid-channel for the benefit of any airmen who were able to get to them after ditching. They were equipped with survival equipment, food and blankets and distress flares and could accommodate up to four men. The floats were marked with red crosses on the sides.

17 WHEN EXPERTS DISAGREE

"It ain't necessarily so."
                    ("Porgy and Bess" – Gershwin)

The final problem facing the Museum researchers now appeared to take the form of almost having too much information on RAF fighter activity, and too little from the ground sources to reach a verdict on who did shoot down Lt Meyer. During December, letters began to arrive from both German and British pilots. Copies of the RAF combat reports made out on the day of action had been sent to W/C Holden, W/C Mackenzie and to AVM Hogan, and provided the right time capsule to revitalise thirty-seven-year-old memories.

W/C Mackenzie was the first to reply from Kenya and agreed that, in the absence of his log book, his earlier letters had been influenced by Mason's time scale in his book "Battle over Britain". He now agreed that the patrol had been the second one of the day, take-off from Kenley being at 13.15 hours on October 7, 1940.

By way of confirmation, he added that he remembered seeing the pilot getting into his dinghy after ditching at or near Hythe as he climbed away back to the 23,000 ft level for his second engagement with 109's some fifteen minutes later. He also recalled that his dental repair job necessitated by his crash landing at Folkestone that day had been done by a gentleman who had already *lunched* rather well, and his breath would have turned any modern day breathaliser green. Mackenzie said, "He attacked my chin with a very unsteady hand . . . and I wondered if he was going to sew my mouth up instead of the gaping chin. However, he appeared to give a concentrated jab and actually made a splendid job of the stitching."

This letter put the pilot of Mackenzie and Hogan's shared 109 in the water around 13.50 hours and fitted in very well with AVM Hogan's letter where he thought that his part had taken place on the second patrol of 501 Squadron on October 7. The only question to be answered was, who was the pilot who ditched to the West of Meyer some ten minutes later – assuming that the first aircraft down was Meyer?

The Dungeness lifeboat had picked that pilot up, but their report did not give his name so the only way to find out was to check the records for the interrogation of German prisoners of war. Here the Museum researchers came up against a brick wall. The Records Office said, "No . . . these records were available ten years ago, but have since been declared sensitive material and closed down."

An approach was then made to Air Historian Peter Cornwell, who provided researchers with a mine of missing information. He had been researching a similar book to "Battle over Britain" about the same time as Mason and had had access to special material now denied to aeronautical archaeologists. These included details of the German Quartermasters' returns for 1940 and the now closed K files or intelligence reports. Generously he agreed to use his files to help the Museum researchers reconstruct the air battle, but only using the K files to give names of pilots and times and places of their crashes.

From his records it was discovered that the pilot picked up by the Dungeness lifeboat was Uffz Bley, and it appeared that he had belonged to 4 LG2, a tactical support unit using 109 e's, and that he had come down in the sea off Greatstone, Kent, just after 14.00 hours on October 7. In his interrogation he said that he ran out of petrol and didn't mention being involved in combat with the RAF. Looking back at Sgt Lacey's combat report, he was in the right area at about the right time on that day and he claimed to have hit the centre radiator of an Me 109 which dived away steeply losing glycol. To researchers it seemed more likely that his victim had been losing petrol and the intriguing possibility emerged that *he* shot up Bley. It was, however, pure speculation.

Peter Cornwell stated firmly that Meyer was in the sea by 13.58 hours on October 7, 1940. Give or take a few minutes each way, his interrogation report showed the time to have been given by him as 14.00 hours. This statement made nonsense of F. K. Mason's report that Meyer was shot down around 10.30 hours that morning. It also made nonsense of the same report that said that Meyer had been shot down by Fl/Lt Holden, whose only combat report that day claimed a 109 shot down in the sea off Dungeness at 10.35 hours. So who did Holden shoot down? Was it Victor Mölders, taking part in the 10.15 hours raid on London? Again, Peter Cornwell stated that Victor Mölders came down near Guestling in Sussex and his interrogation showed him to have force landed about 11.00 hours on October 7. Mölders also denied taking part in a bombing mission and only mentioned being part of a "free hunt". Whether this statement was true or not, Victor Mölders clearly did not take part in the second raid by JG 51 that day, and it was equally clear that Meyer did go up a second time.

Both Peter Cornwell's and F. K. Mason's versions of the German Quartermasters' reports agreed on the number of 109's shot down on October 7, 1940. During the course of the day, seven crashed or forced landed on or around the UK. Two other Me 109 losses were also recorded, one in mid-Channel and the other crashed on landing back at its base in France.

Of these crashes, six of the pilots had been available to RAF interrogation. Peter Cornwell went further and established that the RAF had seventeen fighter units airborne during October 7. Of these units, only 501 and 605 Squadrons were in the right place at the right time to have accounted for Lt Meyer. During the 10.15 raid by JG 51, the reports stated that Holden was credited with a 109 in the sea off Dungeness. During the 13.15 hours raid by JG 51, Sqdn/Ldr Hogan hit a 109 which went into cloud over Ham St. in Kent, but it was losing glycol fast. P/O Mackenzie picked up the same 109 coming out of the cloud at right angles to its previous course and clobbered it again, causing it to slow up rapidly (engine stopped?) and watched it ditch off Hythe and saw the pilot in the sea beside the aircraft.

Museum researchers concluded that Meyer was almost certainly the victim of Hogan and Mackenzie, but were still rather baffled by the original report on events given by the two German pilots, Meyer and Müller. Peter Cornwell thought that much of the blame for this lay with the publication in 1941 of a book by Fritz Forell (a journalist attached to the German armed forces), which stated that Meyer and Victor Mölders were lost on the same mission. Once a statement appears in print, it often becomes part of the memory pattern of those involved in the events recorded. In Meyer's report he quoted freely from the German publication, but in the same report went on to refute that he was flying as Mölders' wingman, but was himself leading the Staffel at the time he was shot down.

Then there was the problem of the Polish pilots mentioned in F. K. Mason's letter to the author (see page 136). The pilot Belc of 303 Squadron claimed a 109 shot down at 13.15 hours on October 7, saying that it went down South of Redhill (Surrey). Peter Cornwell said that the timing and description of events were wrong in so far as the engagement was too far to the West and there was no corroboration from ground sources of this crash.

Peter Cornwell went on to state that a pilot from a Canadian Squadron named Lochnan claimed a Me 109 in flames, but gliding South West from Maidstone at 13.48 hours. This report was also suspect, because in-flight fires were almost impossible to put out and the pilot of the stricken aircraft would almost certainly bale-out. Meyer's aircraft had no signs of an in-flight fire when examined by the Museum staff.

Finally, from his records, it was possible for Peter Cornwell to name all the pilots of the Me 109's that crashed on October 7 and to put the approximate time to each event. JG 51 lost Victor Mölders at 11.00 hours in a crash landing near Guestling (Sussex); Unt/Officer Morschel baled out over Tunbridge Wells at 13.50 hours, and Lt Meyer ditched off Hythe at 13.58 hours approximately. JG 27 lost Uffz Lothar Bartsch, baled out over Headcorn in Kent at 14.00 hours, and 4 LG 2 support unit lost Uffz Bley, who ditched in the sea off Greatstone, Kent, just after 14.00 hours. 5 Staffel of JG 27 lost Uffz Lederer, who force landed near Bedgebury Wood, Cranbrook, at 16.40 hours and Uffz Lege, who crashed near Heathfield, Sussex at 17.30 hours.

The pilot that crashed in mid-Channel was certainly Mackenzie's second victim during the 13.15 hours raid. He was not named in the records but was almost certainly picked up by the Seenotflugkommando.

These pilots were the only 109 losses mentioned in the German Quartermasters' returns for that day. Just for the record, Lt Müller, who witnessed Meyer's last flight, was himself shot down on October 22, 1940. He was flying on an escort mission in 3 Staffel of JG 51 when they dropped bombs on the East End of London, and during the return trip were intercepted by Spitfires. He was hit by the first burst and lost his airscrew and his rudder controls. He dived for cloud cover but was attacked again and his aircraft was hit in many places. He then baled out and came down in the sea off Hastings, Sussex, and was picked up, unwounded and made a prisoner-of-war. The records show that he was shot down jointly by Mungo-Park and Sailor Malan of 74 Squadron.

The only remaining problem for Museum researchers was locating the records of the boat which picked up Lt Meyer and took him to Dover on October 7, and the report of the Lysander pilot who spotted Meyer in the sea at about 16.00 hours. At the time of writing, these reports have not been traced.

On January 8, 1978, two further letters came to curator David Buchanan from Germany. One was from Victor

Mölders, who had survived the war and was still alive and well in Europe, and the other from Lt Meyer.

Mölders said that he was shot down and crash landed at 10.58 hours close to Doleham Farm at Lydham Marshes, near Guestling, Sussex. This letter confirmed the statement by Peter Cornwell.

Lt Meyer said that his memories of events for October 7 were rather fragmented after thirty-seven years, but he recalled a strong premonition that he had that morning, that the day would be a personal disaster for him. He was now sure that the flight took place about midday, preparation commencing around 12.40 hours. He was unable to recall whether he actually flew two missions that morning, but admitted that he thought that the quotation he made from Werner Mölders' book would be of assistance in reconstructing the events of the day.

From his letter, it seemed certain that Museum researchers could deduce that he was leading the second Staffel, and that Victor Mölders was already a prisoner-of-war at the time of take off on Meyer's last mission.

EPILOGUE

Visitors to the Brenzett Aeronautical Museum will soon be able to see the first stage in the reconstruction of Lt Meyer's Messerschmitt BF 109 E 4B. By June, 1978, members hope to have completed the work on the reconstruction of the cockpit area. The wings of the aircraft will still have to be restored although they are in comparatively good condition considering the circumstances. Present plans include the restoration of one complete wing, with the other, suitably pickled, as a reminder of the original condition. The aluminium engine bearers were too badly damaged to be restorable, but the Group are considering ways to remake these vital parts of the structure with steel; aluminium casting being a very expensive item. A DB engine complete, less crank and pistons, will be remounted in the airframe, and the original reduction gearing and airscrew refitted, the blades still showing the effect of the bending stresses from the ditching. The undercarriage will also be fitted and it is hoped to borrow a pair of wheels to replace the original items that were lost due to sea action. The Museum already have a front bulletproof panel and a rear fairing for the cockpit top, and it is also hoped to make a suitable centre canopy.

As far as the rear section of the tail is concerned, the Channel Divers are hoping that their marker buoy will survive the winter months and have plans to attempt recovery of the remainder of the aircraft during the summer of 1978.

The Museum caption for the Messerschmitt will read: –

Messerschmitt BF 109e 4B, werk nr. 4853, flown by Erich B. D. Meyer Leutnant in the 2nd Staffel Jagdeschwader 51 (Mölders). Ditched in the Channel off Hythe, Kent, at 13.58 hours on October 7, 1940, after being attacked by Hurricanes of 501 Squadron over Maidstone.

*　　*　　*

This aircraft was lifted from the sea bed near Hythe, Kent, in July, 1976, as a joint project by the Channel Divers and the Brenzett Aeronautical Museums.

APPENDIX

Aeronautical Archaeologists Turn Crash Detectives

Questions	Group 1	Group 2	Group 3	Group 4	Group 5	Group 6
Operator	Luftwaffe	Meyer	Luftwaffe	Meyer	Hitler	Luftwaffe
Aircraft Type	Me bf 109 4e	Bf 109 E1/B	Me Bf 109 E4	Me 109 E4c	Me 109 E4	Bf 109E 4b
Model	E4	F/B	—	—	—	F/B
Marks	—	4853	—	20/4853	—	Wk No. 4853
Place of Crash	1½ miles ESE of Hythe	Off Hythe	Off Hythe	3 miles off Dymchurch	—	In sea, S of Sandgate
Date	Sept. 1940	Oct. 7 1940	Sept. 7 1940	Sept. 7 1940	Sept., '40	7.10.40
The Investigation						
First events	Sustained damage S of London	—	—	Bombed London	—	See Meyer's combat report
Military Operation	” ”	—	Yes	Yes	—	Yes
Unit		2JG/51				2JG/51
Place of Departure	St. Etienne	Wissant	Wissant	France	—	Wissant, N. France
Reason	Bombing docks	Free chase	Bomber escort	Bombing	—	Bombing London
Radio Transcript	R/T damaged			—		
Time of Operation	Morning	09.30	10.30	—	—	1300 hrs CET
Intended Destination	—	Wissant			—	Wissant
Briefing					—	Attack docks
Other Traffic	RAF			—	—	See map
Accident	—			—	—	
Lat/Long				—	—	
Flying	Sealed 40 to	400 ft				

Field	Report 1	Report 2	Report 3	Report 4	Report 5	Report 6
Crew fate / A/c Damage	POW / Major	POW / Slight	Ditched POW / Damage to cooling radiators	POW / Slight	Slight	POW / Slight
Damage to other aircraft	–	–		–	–	–
Crew	Lt Meyer	Lt E. Meyer	Lt Meyer	Lt Meyer, Erik		Lt Erich Meyer
Age	Not known	Born 25 February 1918				
Licence	No details from any group	"				
Hrs Flown	"	"				
Hrs on type	"	"				
Duty/Rest	"	"				
Aircraft Type	–	S/S Fighter	Messerschmitt			S/S Fighter
Serial No.	–	–	–	–	4853	4853
Date of Construction	–	1938/9	–	–		1939
Reg. Marks	–	2 Staffel	–	–	–	–
C of A	–	–	–	–	–	–
Maintenance Log	No details from any group					
Engine Type	DB 601a	DN 601	DB 601	DB 601	DB 601	DB 601a
Engine No.	–	–	–	Single engine	–	64688
Airframe	Inverted	–	Inverted		–	One/fuselage mounted.
Position	F/armed	–	–	–	–	–
Armament State:						
Guns	2 MG 17 792mm	4 MG 17	–	2 wing/M2 Eng	–	4 X MG 17
Ammunition	7.9mm	7.9mm	7.92mm	7.92mm	–	7.92mm
Bomb load:	–					1 X 250 kg
Commence	250 kg	250 kg	250 kg 250	250 kg		

Questions	Group 1	Group 2	Group 3	Group 4	Group 5	Group 6
Fuel load	–	88 gals	Full/1	–	–	88 gals
How carried	Fus/tank	U/pilot seat		Fus/tank	–	Centre fuselage
Gross Wt A/C	4880lbs	4,680 lbs	5,740 lbs			–
All up wt	5,600		(60lbs permanent ballast in tail)	– RAE report.	5,600lbs	–
Position of C/G	–	Centre of wing (24.8in from L/E) P	L/E of cockpit	Rear/seat		–
Type of fuel	100 Oct Petrol	87 ct P	90 Oct	90oct+oil	–	Petrol
Met. report						
Forecast	–		Clear day			–
Actual	–	4/8ths cloud seeding cumulus				–
Met. at accident actual time	....	10.15 a.m.	....			13.15 hrs.
As above						
light	–		Fair some cloud			Good
Nav. aids	–	Inter/flight	Compass R/T			Compass R/T
Maps or charts	–	R/T				
Communications	–		R/T	R/T		R/T
Flight recorder	–		None			None
The Wreckage						
Location underwater	U/C visible	(Map reference 13755–30425	None	13 National Grid. reference) TR		See divers' report
A/C heading	E.SE	ditto	N/E ditto	S/E		As above
Pitch and lateral attitude	*Inverted nose down*			–		As above
Sketch map observations	Yes	Yes	Yes	Yes		As above
Any part failed (BC) — Indicate what parts damaged, degree of damage when first seen	Rad (I)	Rad/Eng	*No wheels, engine rad*	Ditto		*Cooling system*

iv

Impact forces (LtoH)	Med/Low	Low	Low	Low	–	Med.
A/C attitude on landing	Ditching	Nose up	Level	Ditching	–	–
Relationship of forces found	–	–	Prop blades bent back (all 3)	–	–	–
Any sign of an "in flight" fire	No	Possible	No	No	No	None
Crew Survival						
Was crew found?	Yes	Yes	Yes	Yes		Yes
Where?	In dinghy	In sea	In dinghy	In sea	In sea	In sea
Was he injured?	No	No	No	No	"	None
Condition of seat belt and mountings	Extensive det.	–	Good at time. After 35 yrs bad.	Intact	–	Poor when found
Flight Instruments						
General condition	–	Fair	Poor	Poor	–	Poor
After cleaning	–	–	Fair	"	Cases glass and contents	Needles corroded
Any readings	No	No	No	No	No	Yes
Guns						
Had they been fired?	Yes	Yes	Yes	Yes	–	Yes
Any stoppages?	No	No	No	–	–	Yes, port wing gun had crushed round in breach.
Had bomb been dropped?	Yes	Yes	Yes	Yes	Yes	Yes

Questions	Group 1	Group 2	Group 3	Group 4	Group 5	Group 6
If so, where?	London	–	London docks	–	–	London docks
Engine						
Condition when found	Corroded	Bad	V. bad	Fair	Corroded – bad	Poor
Was damage due to enemy action?	Not visible	No	No	No	No	No
What caused damage?	Sea	Sea	Sea	Sea	Sea	Sea
Were pistons seized?	Yes	Yes	Part	Yes	–	Yes
Was fuel pump working?	No	?	Yes	Yes	–	Yes
Fuel tanks						
Intact	–	–	–	–	–	–
Damaged	–	–	–	–	–	Yes, rotted
Lost	Yes	Yes	–	–	–	–
Contents?	No	No	No	No	No	None
Was cooling system damaged?	Yes	Yes	Yes	Yes	Yes	Yes
If so, how?	Damage to rad by bullets	Ditto	Ditto	Ditto	Ditto	Bullet holes in rads
Oxygen bottles	Empty, cocks open	Yes	Yes	–	–	Empty
Hydraulic system working?	–	Not known	Working at time of crash	–	–	–
Radio	Not found	No	No	No	No	Not yet
Operating frequency	Not known – all groups					

vi

Damage to cockpit

External	Extensive corrosion. Canopy gone	Badly rotted all parts	Badly dented corroded		Only corrosion. glasshouse missing
Internal			Many parts missing		
Flying controls' condition					
No. of units					
Flaps	L/e slats Down	Extended	Ditto	Opened (2) Out	Open locked (2) All flaps
Spoilers	–	2	2 missing	None	None
Ailerons	2 frames no fabric	2 missing	2	–	2
Elevators	No	Not yet	2 no	–	Not yet
Rudder	Not yet	Ditto	One	–	Not yet
Controls					
Engine Throttle	–	Shut	Two	–	One
Switches	–	?	Two	–	One
Rad flaps	No	Missing	–	–	Two
Trims	No	Not yet	–	–	Two
Stick (CC)	Bad corrosion	Ditto	Broken in two, Rotted, held in place by cables.	Ditto	Top intact, stem corroded.
Rudder bar	–	Damaged	Intact	–	–
Pitch Indicator	Airscrew	Missing	No face	–	OK
Compass	No	Fair	No	–	–
ASI	Yes	Missing	Ditto	–	No
Rev counter	–	Fair	Readable	–	–
Altimeter	–	Missing	Not found	–	–
Bank and turn	–	Missing	Not found	–	–
Rate of climb	–	Missing	Not found	–	–
Gyro	–	Missing	Not found	–	–
Gun sight	–	Missing	–	–	–

Questions	Group 1	Group 2	Group 3	Group 4	Group 5	Group 6
Bomb panel	–	–	Yes	–	–	–
Any other instruments?	2 Boost gauges. Rev. c.	–	Bomb arming gear. Fuel pump switch. U/C warning lights. Oxy/Valve boost and temp. gauge	–	–	Boost gauge, water/oil temp. Prop pitch position.
Electrics						
General condition of:						
wiring	–	Poor, corroded.	Good	Good	–	Excellent
busbar	–	–	–	–	–	OK
batteries	–	Not recovered	–	–	–	None
generator	–	Fair	–	Still at sea?	–	None
lights	–	None	–	–	–	One OK
cockpit insp.	–	–	–	–	–	–
Survival Equipment						
Parachute	–	No	–	–	–	No. Believed used by pilot.
Lifejacket	–	–	–	–	–	Yes, four
Dinghy	–	–	–	–	–	,, ,,
Rations	–	–	–	–	–	,, ,,
First aid	–	–	–	–	–	–
Knife	–	–	–	–	–	–
Pistol	–	–	–	–	–	–
Flare pistol	–	–	–	–	–	–
Cartridges	–	–	4 in rack rotted	rotted	–	Yes, four
Distress beacon	–	–	–	–	–	No
Maps	–	–	–	–	–	No

Question					
Why was U/C down and locked?	Failed hydraulics, air in tyres, raised U/C?	–	Believe A/C hydr. shot up causing pressure loss.	Debatable	*Air in tyres lifted out U/C centre legs after oil pressure lost.*
What happened to wheels?	Corroded off	Ditto	Ditto	Ditto	*Magnesium rots quickly. Mag. centre rotted away.*
Why did tail break off?	Trawler	Lift	Armour plate weakened corroded structure.	Suction weight of sand.	*Weight of sand and corrosion when lifted.*
Why did engine bearers break?	Corrosion	Ditto	Ditto	Ditto	Magnesium corroded lift stresses. All magnesium corrosion took about 5 years (?)
Airscrew pitch	22.5° to 90°	10.2ft dia. 3 blades	U/P metal		
Why did airscrew separate from engine?	Corrosion	Ditto	Corrosion	? Fracture on prop hitting sea.	*Magnesium casting on front of engine*
Where is cockpit canopy?	Ejected by pilot	*Broken during recovery*	Pilot action	Still at sea	*Lost at time of crash landing. Dropped back in sea after examination.*
Where are the guns?	–	At sea	At sea	At sea	
If pilot survived, who picked him up?	*Dover MTB*	ASR boat	*Dover ASR*	Dungeness lifeboat	Dover lifeboat
At what time?	–	Late afternoon	–	–	*1600 hours GMT*
What do you think happened to the aircraft on this day?	*MG fire caused engine to seize near UK coast. Pilot ditched and used dinghy.*	Don't know	No comment	Shot down	*See pilot's report*

Conclusions from Group Reports

(*In the charts shown on pages ii to ix items in italics represent correct answers.*)

The six groups contained, on average, three members. Group 1 had the leader of the divers' team. Group 3 contained the expert on instruments, and Group 6 had one member who had access to historic records. Nearly all members were present during the beaching and some were involved in specialist jobs, like instrument cleaning, controls examination and the like. A few members used their imagination to reason their conclusions, and one or two made quite illogical replies. The sketch maps of the underwater wreck were all similar, showing that considerable attention had been paid to the divers' reports in 1974 to 1976. The way in which the questions were answered showed some confusion as to the subject, Question 1 being the classic example.

In summary, the joint group report would suggest that the aircraft was operated by the Luftwaffe. The aircraft type was an Me bf 109E 4b with serial marks 4853, sub-contractor Arado. Only Group 6 remembered the engine number – 64688 – and two groups recorded the engine with the suffix 'a' after the number 601. On the engine position, Groups 1, 3 and 6 agreed that it was mounted inverted. On the armament state, Group 1 only recorded wing mounted guns, all other groups recorded the additional engine mounted twin guns. There was total agreement that the ammunition used was 7.9 mm and that the guns were still loaded. All groups were agreed that the 250 kg bomb had been carried at the start of the operation, and, equally, all were certain that there was no bomb on the aircraft when salvaged. The influence of the pilot's report was clear in this instance. On the fuel load carried, Groups 2 and 6 said 88 gallons, all groups agreed that the fuel was petrol, and several groups hazarded a guess at the octane rating, 90 being the favourite. The position of the fuel tank produced a problem for all groups, as it was not found in the wreck, having corroded away completely. Most groups said it was fuselage mounted, and Group 2 thought it to have been under the pilot's seat so, as the tank was L-shaped, all groups were half right.

The gross weight of the aircraft was given in German and RAE reports as 5,600 lbs. Groups 1 and 2 quoted the dry weight of the aircraft without taking into account the weight of the fuel and ammunition. Group 3 was just overweight at 5,740 lbs. No one knew that some early marks of Me 109 E's carried 60 lb ballast in the tail unit, as this part of the aircraft was still in the sea. No doubt members will notice the difference when they try lifting the salvaged tail. Regarding the position of the C/g, not unnaturally they had no information on this vital statistic. Group 2 was nearest, quoting the centre of the main wing. Group 4 said that it was behind the pilot's seat, but in that position the A/C would have never got off the ground being totally nose-heavy. The correct answer was 24.8 inches from the leading edge of the wing. When asked to predict the weather on the day of the operation, Groups 2 and 3 were correct according to historic met. reports for 1940. Group 6 said it was good (it wasn't raining) which was fair enough. Asked about navigation aids for the pilot, Groups 2, 3 and 6 got it right quoting the aircraft compass and interflight radio. Groups 1, 2, 4 and 5 rightly ducked the question which asked if a flight recorder was fitted. Groups 3 and 6 got it right, stating that one was not carried. (They did not come into general use until the 1960's.) All groups agreed that no maps or charts were found.

On the burning question of the correct location of the wreckage, Group 1 with the divers' leader said it was located by the undercarriage being extended, which was correct, but none of the groups remembered the map reference (the museum's map king being absent from the meeting). The correct answer was MR TR 13. 13755–30425 National grid. The aircraft heading underwater was given by Group 1 as E.SE, which was right. The other groups who had not been down to look ducked the question. Group 6 wisely said "see divers' report". Asked to describe the attitude of the wreckage underwater, all groups knew that the aircraft was inverted and slightly nose down. All groups provided a sketch map to prove this and were in total agreement, so the divers had got that information across at an early stage in the operation. Asked about the impact forces at the ditching, all groups said that they were medium to low in effect on the airframe.

Asked what the aircraft attitude (in flight) had been at the moment of ditching, five said, "level flight", and Group 3 said "nose up". (As far as is known, no members of the groups had pilot experience.) Asked to comment on the effect of forces in ditching, only Group 3 commented that the propeller blades had been bent back. Asked if there had been any in-flight fire, all groups except 2 said none. Group 2 just said "possible", but did not offer any evidence. All groups agreed that the pilot was uninjured. The double question asking about the condition of the seat belts and mountings was answered in the singular by all groups. Group 1 said "extensive deterioration", Groups 2 and 3 answered, "Good at ditching, bad after thirty-five years", Group 4 said "intact", and Group 6 said "poor when found". (The belts had rotted away and the mountings showed no evidence of stress loadings and were slightly corroded.)

The groups' joint observations on the condition of the flight instruments indicated that everyone had taken a good look during the salvage work. None were readable. Asked about the condition of the guns when found, all groups were unanimous that they had all been fired. When asked if any of the guns had stoppages, only Group 6 answered that the port wing gun had a crushed round in the breach. All groups agreed that a bomb had been carried, and Groups 1, 3 and 6 all knew that the bomb had been dropped in the London area, probably on the docks. This was surprising as the only evidence that a bomb had been carried came from the pilot's report, and he did not indicate where the bomb fell. He just said, "We dropped the bombs too late." As the German Groups were being attacked by British fighters at the time and were at 20,000 feet, it was an even bet that the formation bombing was widely scattered and the bombs could have dropped within a radius of ten miles of the target. No one seems to have traced any confirmation of the raid and time with ARP records.

Asked to describe the condition of the engine when salvaged, all groups except 4 described it as badly corroded. Group 4 said "fair". Asked what had caused the damage, all groups blamed the sea action. Asked if the pistons were seized, all groups except 3 answered "yes". Group 3, with commendable caution, said "part seized", having understood the implication of the bent propeller blades. When asked if the fuel pump was working, Group 1 said "no", Group 2 "didn't know", Groups 3, 4 and 6 said "yes". (Again, referring to the pilot's report, he said, "I was now at a height of 400 mtrs . . . so I controlled the aircraft with a standing propeller to the Channel . . ." meaning that the engine was not turning from a height of 400 mtrs.' It would have been correct to say that the fuel pump was working up to this point. We must assume that he would have switched off the engine after it seized to reduce the risk of fire. This was a very serious risk at that point in the flight. The condition of the fuel tank was described by all groups as lost and the cause correctly ascribed to the sea. All groups agreed that the contents had been lost.

All groups were agreed that the cooling system had been damaged and that there had been bullet holes in the radiators.

The condition of the oxygen bottles was good, according to Groups 1, 2, 3 and 6, and Groups 1, 2 and 6 added that the cocks were open and the bottles empty. No one remembered if the bottles had an inspection date stamped on them, although Len Green, in a previous statement, said that he found a date stamp and had thought it to be August, 1940.

Asked if the hydraulic systems had been working, all groups except 3 said, "Don't know". Group 3 said, "Working at the time of the crash", a good qualified answer.

Asked about the radio and frequency set, all groups except 6 said it was not found. Group 6, in an optimistic note, said "not yet", no doubt bearing in mind Jess's promise to find the tail unit where the radio was located.

The state of the cockpit was described generally as "damaged and badly corroded"; Groups 3 and 6 noted the significance of the missing glasshouse.

The flying controls had been of interest to all groups and they were all in agreement that the slots (L/E) had been extended and locked. On the condition of the landing flaps, Group 1 said they were down; Group 2 said there were two and Group 3 said that both were missing; Group 4 said there were none and Group 6 said both flaps were present. The Group 1 answer is interesting, as the divers' reports had said that the flaps were loose in their mounting and extended.

The ailerons were given by all groups as two present, and Groups 1 and 2 commented that the fabric covering had rotted. All groups agreed that they hadn't seen the rudder and elevators in the wreckage brought ashore. Groups 1 and 6 both said "not yet", indicating hope for the future diving plans.

Other controls found in the cockpit presented some problems, as identifying the controls meant knowledge of the usage. All groups identified the throttle, and Group 2 indicated that it was in the closed position when found. The radiator flap controls were identified only by Group 6 and the trim wheels also identified by Group 6. All groups agreed that the control column had been badly corroded and Group 3 indicated that it was broken in half and held in place by the control cables.

Curiously, the rudder bar was intact, but only Groups 2, 3 and 6 mentioned this. The instrument state was largely directed to Len Green (Group 3) and he said that there was a compass without a face, an altimeter which was readable, a bomb panel and also bomb aiming gear, fuel pump switch, U/C warning lights, oxygen valve switch, and a boost and temperature gauge. Group 6 mentioned additionally a boost gauge, water/oil temperature gauge and a prop position indicator.

Regarding the electrics used, four of the groups described the wiring as good and Group 6 said "excellent and capable of carrying current". Asked about the condition of the busbar, Group 6 said it was "OK". Batteries were not found, said all groups, and there was no claim made for the finding of a generator. Only Group 6 noticed the one cockpit inspection lamp.

Survival equipment raised important aspects of the pilot's report. All groups said that it was not found. No one had found the dinghy or the lifejacket. This was also true of the rations, knife, first aid gear, flare pistol and the pilot's pistol. Some four flare cartridges were found in the rack according to Groups 3 and 6.

There was no distress beacon found either.

The groups were then asked to express an opinion on why the undercarriage was found in the down and locked position. Group 1 said "the hydraulics failed, and the air in the tyres raised the undercarriage". Groups 2 and 3 said that they believed that the hydraulic system had been shot up causing a pressure loss. Group 4 thought it was very debatable and Group 6 said that the air in the tyres lifted the U/C legs out after oil pressure was lost. No one knew if the system was fitted with "up-locks" as well as "down-locks".

When asked what happened to the wheels, all groups agreed that the magnesium centre of the hub had rotted away fairly quickly. This raised the question which rotted first, the wheels, allowing the tyres to float away, or the hydraulic system, allowing the oil to escape?

Do dead aircraft raise their legs in extremis?

There is known evidence that they do, but only under certain circumstances. First, a ditching on water must be made successfully. Second, the aircraft must be nose heavy and follow the normal laws of aerodynamics by sinking, nose first, then slowly becoming inverted and continuing the water-borne bunt, finishing up on the sea bed with the airframe intact but inverted.

To continue with this common factor's condition, the aircraft must have a system of undercarriage retraction that involves the use of hydraulics, and the "up and down locks" must be spring loaded. (These locks have the sole function of retaining the undercarriage in the up or down position only, and the legs are secured by a simple latch device.) Ideally, the fairings or U/C doors are not load bearing structures and serve only as a part of the streamlining function to the wings or fuselage.

With these conditions fulfilled, the stage is then set for the start of a curious set of conditions of change which relate only to salt water submersion.

It is normal to ditch an aircraft with the U/C retracted, as a lowered U/C is an open invitation to flip the aircraft over onto its back at the first water contact, which may usually be made at speeds around 100 mph. Such a condition makes the escape of the crew very difficult, or even impossible. After the aircraft has sunk and is resting on the sea bed inverted, the next part in the chain of events has already started. The up locks have been freed by the two or three hard slaps on the U/C fairings by the water during ditching, and the admission of water inside the wheel housings, cushioning the last shock which prevents the locks re-engaging.

Thus, the U/C is free to move, so far as the locks are concerned, but because of the hydraulic fluid retaining the position of the mechanism, it does not do so. The fairings usually attached to the U/C legs are almost always torn away by the water impact, and aircraft fitted with doors subjected to forces well outside those considered in the design stress calculations usually collapse.

If the aircraft has sunk in fairly shallow water (up to 50 ft) a change occurs in the forces acting on the tyres, which are normally inflated to a fairly low pressure, and they now develop a very strong upward force on the U/C legs.

Because of the fluid in the hydraulic system being retained, the legs cannot move far in an upward position, but just far enough to prevent the up locks re-engaging.

Now the action of the salt in the sea water commences, small quantities entering the hydraulic system by way of the vent hole in the fluid reservoir, thus commencing the breakdown of the whole system by corrosion. The time factor varies with the metals used in the construction of the system. The salt water also gets to work on the magnesium alloy used in the construction of the U/C wheels, again a time variable reaction, but usually much longer than the widening of the hole for venting in the hydraulic fluid reservoir. After sufficient hydraulic fluid has leaked away, the undercarriage legs are free to move upward in their normal working arc, and do so, because of the action of the upward forces on the tyres. When the fully open position of the U/C is reached, then the down locks operate, holding the U/C in the fully open position. The corrosion continues on the wheel rims and, after a further period of time, the high corrosion rate allows the wheel rims to implode under the extra tyre pressure and the tyres free themselves from the seating and float to the water surface. The aircraft may be found after the passing of several years with the U/C legs extended and the wheel axles without the wheels.

The foregoing explanation cannot work if the aircraft is submerged in greater depths of water, as the greatly increased water pressure would either deform or burst the tyres, thus removing the forces necessary to extend the undercarriage.

Several examples of this phenomenon have been found underwater by divers. The Me 109 E4 which ditched off Dymchurch Redoubt in 1940 and was recovered by a sub-aqua diving team in 1976 is a classic case. A further example, also a Me 109 E4 is still underwater (at about 80 ft) off the Kent coast. Near Portsmouth, a Vampire ditched and was recovered by the divers, also in the systemic equivalent of *rigor mortis*.

Author

The Royal Aircraft Establishment, Farnborough – A Viewpoint

In a letter to the author from a spokesman at the RAE, it was said: —

"We now come to the matter of the undercarriage found to be down, i.e. sticking up like the legs of a dead insect with the aircraft inverted and buried in the seabed silt to the lower surfaces of the wings with the fuselage full of mud at a depth below low water at around 7 fathoms. Recently, I saw some photographs of aircraft much later than WW2 fighters after they had been retrieved from a watery grave. They also had their undercarriages down and one assumes that they did not enter in this fashion. One does not wish to commence a dissertation on the behaviour of aircraft in the systemic equivalent of *rigor mortis*, but after discussions with various people, it appears that some time after ditching the hydraulic system empties and corrosion allows escape of the hydraulic fluid that is locking components in position. Here one should interject that positive mechanical lock-ups may not have been used, as it was common for German aircraft in WW2, if hit in the hydraulic system, to lower their undercarriage legs inadvertently. Furthermore, up-locks can cause trouble in not permitting an undercarriage to be lowered when it is selected so. This last was a worry in an air force with its first generation of retractable U/C high performance aircraft which were all too often landing with their undercarriages up because the pilots forgot. Then following the release, the flotation offered by the tyres and the forces exerted by the sea bed currents eventually bring the leg to the vertical where the over top dead centre mechanical lock arrangement fixes it there. The sea bed currents in time remove the leg fairings and tyres, even if corrosion has not already done so. As mentioned during your visit, aircraft can move a considerable distance between ditching and settling, thus these 109's may have entered the sea several miles from where the diving team located them."

What the law had to say

In January, 1977, a local newspaper printed a report about forty-three motorists coming up before the local JPs on charges of obstruction on the coast road at Dymchurch, Kent, in July, 1976. Police told the magistrates that it caused an hour of total traffic chaos, because an aircraft recovery group had been salvaging a wartime Messerschmitt from the sea. It was said that passing motorists had abandoned their cars at the roadside to go to the beach front to watch the salvage. One motorist was quoted as saying that there were no restrictive notices and he assumed that it was all right to park. Police Inspector Young (prosecuting) said, "If a line of vehicles obstructed the main road, then they could expect to be prosecuted for obstruction." This defendant was discharged by the magistrates. The newspaper report didn't say what happened to the other forty-two cases.

Wing Commander Mackenzie, DFC, AFC, AMBIM, RAF (retired)

During the 1940 period he was serving as a P/O in 501 Squadron of 2 Group, and after the Battle he moved up to Colerne operating day and night with the new "night fighter" concept. He was subsequently posted to 247 Squadron, night fighter and intruder Hurricanes at Predannick in Cornwall as a flight commander.

Later he was shot down by flak, whilst blitzing Morlaix airfield in Brittany at night. This "intruder type" operation, was usually reserved for moonlight nights when there were no UK air raids in the Western sector.

After his crash, he made his way to the coast, stole a small fishing boat and started out for the UK, but was picked up by a German E boat when about 15 miles out to sea near the island of St Batz. He spent the rest of the war as a POW in Germany and Poland, keeping himself occupied as a tunneller and escapist.

After the war, he returned to the RAF and continued serving as an instructor and later went operational on Jets. He also served for a spell on the staff of the Ministry of Defence until he retired prematurely to become the Deputy Commander of the Zambian Air Force. At a later stage of his career, he became managing director of a large charter company in Kenya, having acquired a commercial pilot's licence. He is currently working as an aviation and engineering consultant in Nairobi, Kenya.

He also served as Hon Sec, of the Battle of Britain Fighter Pilots' Association for five years when he was still serving in the UK. He said that he still attends the annual reunions whenever possible.

Wing Commander Eustace Holden, OBE, DFC, RAF (retired)

When Sqdn/Ldr Hogan, left 501 Squadron in November, 1940, W/C Holden (then Sqd/Ldr) took over command of 501. He had some interesting things to say about the quality of fighter pilots during the Battle of Britain and thought that in most squadrons you could divide the pilots into two groups: Those that were the natural killers and those that went along on the raids as passengers.

The Killers were usually splendid shots and were experts at deflection shooting. They usually asked more of their aircraft and were not necessarily the best pilots, but they got results. They did not come from any particular type of person, being either introverted or extroverted and came to flying from many different backgrounds.

His story of three of his squadron chasing a JU 88 back over the Channel from Lyme Regis illustrates the problems involved in trying to shoot down a very low flying aircraft. He said: "There were three of us. I missed him in my first attack and I could see my bullets hitting the water. My number 2 had a go and unfortunately hit the water and killed himself.

There was a heavy cross wind which put our aims off a bit so I just sat behind him, blazing away to no effect and his rear gunner was firing continuously at me at the same time. However he made it back to the French coast, unloading his bombs as he crossed, but they didn't go off."

W/C Holden stayed with 501 Squadron till 1941 and then went out to Africa, having first converted to twin engined aircraft. In Lagos he was O/C Dispatch Flight for seventeen months. At the end of that tour he came back to London at the Air Ministry and then went on to Staff College. He was then posted out to the Far East; places like Singapore and Hong Kong and returned to the UK in 1947.

He retired from the Force in 1964.

Lt Erich B. O. Meyer, Pilot of "The Reluctant Messerschmitt".

Born Feb 25, 1918, in East Prussia.
Enlisted in Luftwaffe, April, 1936, as Flieger-Ersatz-Abteilung in Neukuren. October, 1936, transferred to flying training School at Jueterbog, Nr Berlin. August, 1939, promoted 2nd Lt and posted to fighter school at Schleibheim near Munich, for fighter pilot training. In January, 1940, he transferred to Jagd-Ergeanzungs Gruppe to provide protection to the synthetic rubber factories in Leuna. In May, 1940, he was transferred to the combat troops in Jever. JG 51 was formed from this group. In June 1940 he was posted to Den Helder in Holland with the role of intercepting RAF reconnaisance flights over the Islands and North Sea.

Had his first victory at night (unconfirmed) after intercepting a RAF aircraft over the sea. On his return to base he was nearly shot down by German flak. His next move was to Wissant, France, at the nearby airfield. He claims to have flown over 300 missions against England averaging four trips a day.

Before his final flight on October 7, 1940, he had 14 officially confirmed victories and was the holder of: Eisernes Kreuz Second and First Class, the Deutches Kreuz, the Goldere Jagdflieger-Frontflugspanne, and the Silverner Jagdflieger – Ehrenpokal of Reischmarchall.

Handling Tests on the Me 109

During September, 1940, the Royal Aircraft Establishment published a secret report on a captured Messerschmitt BF 109E. The report described handling and manoeuvrability tests after being flown by three pilots of the aerodynamic Flight. Additionally, a number of flights were flown in mock combat with Hurricanes and Spitfires, the latter aircraft being piloted by operational pilots drawn from several squadrons of Fighter Command.

The report drew attention to a number of shortcomings in the combat flight performance of the Me 109E. Manoeuvrability at high airspeeds was said to be seriously curtailed by the heaviness of the controls and the high wing loading caused it to stall readily under high normal accelerations which resulted in a poor turning circle. The minimum radius of turn, without loss of height at 12,000 ft full throttle, was calculated at 885 ft on the Me 109 compared with 696 ft on the Spitfire.

Absence of a rudder trimmer on the Me 109 was described as a severe handicap at high speeds, as there is a large change of directional trim with speed. The report described the aircraft as being too stable longitudinally for a fighter.

The DB 601 direct injection engine came in for very favourable comment as pilots found it impossible to choke the engine when opening the throttle and also the engine did not splutter or stop when subjected to negative G.

The cockpit came in for some adverse criticism, being described as far too cramped for comfort, being too narrow and with insufficient headroom.

The main flying controls were described as good, but the raised position of the rudder bar made for far too reclining an attitude of the pilot, putting extra weight on the small of the back. (W/C Mackenzie said in 1977 that the reclining rake of the seat and the raising of the rudder bar enabled the Luftwaffe pilots to withstand higher G loading than RAF pilots.) The Farnborough report does not mention this factor.

MEMBERS OF THE DIVING TEAM
The Channel Divers
1974 to 1976

Names of divers who took part in operation Me 109 from start to finish:

Team Leader: G. M. (Jess) Henderson
G. J. Bradberry (Graham 'Little')
D. Casey
G. Hayes (Graham 'Big')

Divers who helped out during the operations:

M. Henderson
W. Stevens
A. Wood
J. Reid
B. Stevens

Divers who came up specially from the Wells Diving Group for the beaching:

P. Poll
G. Greenslade

The team of divers made 188 boat runs.

Sea miles covered totalled 282.

The contents of 209 air bottles were consumed (12,480 cu ft).

Petrol used by the inflatables between 1974/76 totalled 172 gallons.

Fuel for the Coventry Climax used totalled 22 gallons.

A provisional estimate of the sand and clay removed to free the wreck was 22,000 cu ft.

THE BRENZETT AERONAUTICAL MUSEUM TEAM

(Ashford and Tenterden Recovery Group)   1976 to 1978

David Buchanan.   Group leader. (Chairman).
Leonard Green.   Vice Chairman.
Audrey Buchanan.   Secretary.
Dennis Timms.   Treasurer.
Rodney Collins.
John Elgar Whinney.   Map King.
Roland Freeman.
Peter Foote.   German research on Me 109.
Richard Hukins.
James Pope.
Malcolm Timms.
David Gould.
David Ford.
Bernard Killick.
William (Bill) Hamblyn.
Robert Cole.

The total cost of the sea-lift of the Me 109 at Dymchurch in 1976 was £638.80p for fuel, materials, air for the divers and the hire of the trawler for towing and the final lift.

All manual labour, the shore winch lorry, JCB digger and the final transport of the aircraft by low loader, were free of charge.

ACKNOWLEDGEMENTS

The author, the museum team and the divers wish to acknowledge the help of the undermentioned firms, organisations and individuals in the recovery of the Messerschmitt from the Redoubt at Dymchurch: —

Messrs. E. H. Brown & Sons – for the loan of the low loader and the steam cleaning plant.
Messrs. Burmah Castrol Ltd. – for the gift of special oils and for technical advice.
H.M. Coast Guards – for historic records, and the work of their rescue services.
Mr. A. J. E. Egan (Servo Electronic Sales, Lydd) – for the gift of special equipment.
F/Lt R. Hall, DFC, and members of 354 Squadron ATC – for beach duties by ATC cadets.
The Kent County Constabulary – for their work in crowd control.
The Ministry of Defence S4c (Air) – for help with historic records and documentation.
Capt S. Moore, Junior Leaders (RE) Dover – for special help at the beaching.
The Southern Water Authority – for loan of the beaching site.
Mr. K. Wood (Hythe Plant Services) – for the loan of the JCB and lorry.
To H.M. Receiver of Wrecks – for easing the problems of salvage rights.
Messrs. Walker Bros. – for the loan of the compressors.

Historical information.

P. D. Cornwell.
Air Vice Marshal H. A. V. Hogan, CB, DFC.
Wing Commander E. Holden, OBE, DFC.
Wing Commander K. W. Mackenzie, DFC, AFC.
Herr H. Kirchner.
Herr E. Meyer.
Herr K. Müller.
Herr V. Mölders.